Little Fires Everywhere:

Pandemic, Protest, Politics and Power

A Pentecost Sermon Series

By

Rev. Valencia Edner, M.S., M.Th.

&

Rev. Dr. Van Carl Williams, D.Min.

Little Fires Everywhere:

Pandemic, Protest, Politics and Power

A Pentecost Sermon Series

Copyright © 2021

By

Rev. Valencia Edner
&
Rev. Dr. Van Carl Williams

TABLE OF CONTENTS

INTRODUCTION

The messages in this volume were delivered from the pulpits of empty sanctuaries, and shared through social media, to speak to people living amidst a global pandemic, public protests, and social strife on streets around the world in 2020.

Shortly after novel Corona virus infections were discovered in the United States of America in February 2020, local government agencies across the country issued executive orders mandating persons only leave their homes for essential services—like grocery shopping and doctor visits—or if they were deemed essential workers of health care and select other fields. In-person social gatherings were limited to less than 100 participants, then to a few dozen participants, and eventually to no more than 10 or 15 participants in many parts of the country. These "shelter in place" or "shutdown" protocols shuttered schools, businesses, restaurant dining rooms, dance clubs, banquet facilities, large meeting rooms, and a host of other venues—including houses of worship. Some Christians playfully opined that all church members were now on the "Sick and Shut-In List" as many followed recommendations to stay at home to help reduce spread of the Corona virus.

In African American (and other) communities, sheltering-in-place was not viable—on May 25, 2020—as video and details emerged about the death of George Floyd in Minneapolis, MN. A local shop owner had accused Floyd of using a counterfeit twenty-dollar bill to pay for services in his store. Derek Chauvin, a responding officer, was captured on cell phone video pinning a handcuffed George Floyd, face down on the pavement, with his knee on Floyd's neck for eight minutes and forty-six seconds. He was aided by two other officers in restraining Floyd, while another prevented onlookers from intervening. The final words heard spoken by Floyd according to the video and eyewitness accounts were "I can't breathe," and calling the name of his late mother, before his body became motionless in the last two minutes of the video.

The event sparked immediate protests in Minneapolis which quickly spread to hundreds of cities across the country. Tens of thousands of protesters, male and female, of all ethnicities (many wearing masks as a precaution against corona virus infection) took to the streets with raised voices and pumping fists, chanting "Justice for George" declaring "Black Lives Matter" and calling for greater police accountability and policing reform. Several cities called up the National Guard to quell protests; curfews were imposed but largely ignored, and a number of businesses and other structures were set afire by some non-peaceful protesters. In short order, the protests became international as more than 60 countries saw gatherings supporting the Black Lives Matter Movement and denouncing police brutality and racism in America and in their countries.

However, the synagogue, the mosque, and (especially) the Black Church sanctuary could not be the meeting place for persons at the forefront of the protest to hear inspiring messages reinforcing their just cause. Church fellowship halls could not be converted into organizing spaces to strategically plan the work of civil unrest and social engagement. The messaging, the organizing, the strategizing had all moved online. Social media platforms, in the wake of the Corona virus "shutdown" had officially become for the current movement, what the Black Church had been for the Civil Rights Movement. To be sure, during the "shutdown," many churches migrated to social media and other digital platforms to create virtual worship experiences with the trappings of worship online—preaching, singing, praying, fellowship—but the voice of the Black Church and the Black Church preacher—intoning the heart of protest, the hope of the protesters, and vision of God for all people—was largely missing.

During a casual conversation, God laid it on our hearts to speak to our virtual congregations about the social unrest unfolding in front of us—not in a manner that condemned the protesters, but in a manner that captured the prophetic nature of the protests. We were (and are) convinced that God was at work in the events of 2020, calling for a global reckoning for past and present injustices, and revolution leading to a more equitable and just future. It occurred to us, then, as no coincidence that the fires of protest were ignited in the days leading up to the Christian celebration of Pentecost Sunday—hailed as the birthday of the Christian Church. The inaugural Pentecost celebration of Acts 2 is characterized by the Spirit of God appearing as tongues of fire and lighting upon followers of Jesus who were waiting for Jesus' promise of divine empowerment to be fulfilled in them.

In addition to the intersecting symbolism of the fires ignited during social protests and the scripture's Pentecost account, the streaming service HULU aired a miniseries adaptation of Celeste Ng's novel Little Fires Everywhere in March. The miniseries easily became one of the most watched of the season. We, like countless others, found ourselves discussing it on social media, in ZOOM conferences, with family members, friends, and strangers. The "fires" motif both in the title and in the miniseries, provided not only a parallel cultural hermeneutic, but shared themes with present day protests, protestors, and those who were present on the inaugural New Testament narrative of Pentecost.

Our task, then, became to braid the parallel strands of fires into a single stream of proclamation in the Black Church tradition. Each week we talked about our "braiding"—the premise, the process, the points—of our messages—where we converged and where we diverged. These messages are not exercises in, or exemplars of, expository, narrative, or any other school of preaching. If you attempt to read them as such, you will miss their messages. These are two preachers attempts to articulate what we heard God saying to us in an unprecedented era of American and world existence that will not soon be forgotten.

Pentecost Sunday

Something's about to Happen

It is not for you to know the times or periods… But you will receive Power when the Holy Spirit has come upon you.
Acts 1:7-8

For 3 months, we have been living through the COVID-19 Pandemic in America. As a result, in-person instruction has ended in many school districts with more than a quarter of the school year remaining. Restaurants have shuttered their dining rooms. Many corporations have transitioned employees into working from home. Over 40 million people have filed for unemployment. Some states, including Texas, claim they are "ready to reopen" but, many people and places are still in a state of being shutdown.

During this shut down, with no place to go, and very few things to do, many pass their extended time at home watching television or binge-watching shows on Netflix, Hulu, and other streaming services. One of the highest rated and recommended shows currently streaming on Hulu is an 8-part miniseries called "Little Fires Everywhere."The miniseries is based on a novel of the same name written by Celeste Ng—an American-born woman of Chinese descent.

The miniseries centers on the relationship of Elena and Mia. Elena is a white, well-off, woman, wife, and mother living (what appears to be) a picture-perfect life with her family in the exclusive Ohioan neighborhood of Shaker Heights. Mia is a Black, nomadic single mother of a 15-year old daughter named Pearl. She comes to Shaker Heights, takes a job as a waitress, moves into Elena's rental property, and becomes Elena's family's maid.

Is Art Imitating Life or Life Imitating Art?

"Little Fires Everywhere" is a story about race and class,

politics and privilege, motherhood, mistakes, and misery. It is a story about identity and history, ownership and oppression, control, chaos, and trying to keep it all together.

I do not want to give many plot details because some of you may be currently watching or have the miniseries on your "watch list." However, I can tell you that the story begins at the end. It begins with Elena's house, the Richard's family's house, engulfed in fire—literally. Flames are shooting through the roof. Smoke-clouds are billowing into the night sky. Firefighters are on the scene contending with the blaze. A fire department investigator then approaches and informs Elena that the fire was an act of arson. It was set intentionally.

After beginning with the ending, the storyline rewinds eleven months to show viewers how Mia and Elena met, and the subsequent events that led to the fire. In other words, the storyline begins by showing viewers *what* happened, then carries us on a trip to understand the who, the how, the where, and the why the fire started in the first place.

This storytelling device mirrors what is currently happening in these "Divided States of America."Right now the country is on fire—literally on fire. There are fires in Minneapolis, Minnesota, Fires in Chicago and Detroit, Cincinnati and Boston, New York, Washington and Richmond. There are fires in Atlanta and Des Moines, Denver and Louisville, Kansas City and Oakland, San Jose, and Los Angeles. There are fires in Portland and Eugene, Oregon; Phoenix; Austin, and right here in Dallas. If you have watched a national news outlet, or visited social media, over the last few days, then you should know that there are—literally—little fires everywhere. Not only in the few cities that I mentioned— everywhere. Protesters, rioters, looters, marchers, angry people, frustrated people, confused people—marching in the streets, turning over cars, breaking windows, raising their signs, their fists, and their voices—there are little fires everywhere.

And much like in Celeste Ng's book, and the mini-series of the same name, there are those who see the fires blazing and wonder how they started. News reporters say that the fires started in response to the murder of George Floyd—the Black man in Minneapolis, MN, who died after a white police officer, Derek Chauvin, held him, handcuffed and face down on the ground, with his knee in Floyd's neck for nearly nine minutes. The event was witnessed by civilians, recorded by onlookers, and shared across social and news media platforms. I submit, however, that the little fires everywhere are bigger than George Floyd.

It's about More than George Floyd

On March 13, 2020, Brenna Taylor, was killed by police officers who entered her house, in the middle of the night, executing a no-knock search warrant in Louisville, Kentucky. Police were at the wrong address and the person for whom they were looking was not a relative of Breonna Taylor's. What is more, the person for whom the police were looking had already been arrested and was in custody. Yet Breonna Taylor's body was riddled with multiple gunshot wounds because police "made a mistake."On February 23, 2020, Ahmaud Arbery, a Black man jogging in Brunswick, GA was hunted, accosted, shot, and killed by two white men who had their white friend film the event.

These protests and fires are about more than George Floyd. They are about the Botha Jeans, and the Tamir Rices, and the Atatiana Jeffersons, and the Sandra Blands, and the Trayvon Martins, and the Eric Garners, and the Michael Browns, and the Rakia Boyds, and the Freddie Grays, and the Philando Castilles, and the Charleston Nine, and the hundreds and thousands of other Black and Brown men, women, and children who have been killed by law enforcement officials, racist neighbors, and self-deputized cops while simply trying to live their lives.

They're about the fact that as of this morning over 105,000people have died from Corona virus in America—that's more than any other country in the world—and most of the deaths and new cases are People of Color—but white people wielding governmental power don't care—they just want the country "reopened," and the economy to recover.

They're about the rhetoric of Donald Trump, the Republican

Party, and racists everywhere, who do not care about Black and Brown skin, the welfare of Black and Brown lives, or the shedding of innocent Black and Brown blood! They are about America never confessing or repenting of its sin of slavery, systemic racism, and white privilege, and the way America still propagates those same systems today.

That's why there are little fires everywhere—because America has proven to be hypocritical—intoning liberty while espousing slavery, intoning equality while espousing white privilege and elitism. America habitually demonstrated that she does not give a damn about her people, so more and more of her people are showing that we don't give a damn about her police, or her property, her principles, her practices, or her policy makers either!

Prose and Protests Meet Pentecost

The symbolism cannot be overlooked, that while there are little fires everywhere in America, today is Pentecost Sunday in the Christian church, and in the foundational Pentecost text there are also little fires everywhere. Acts 2:1-3 says a group of Jesus' followers were in one place, with one purpose, and suddenly fires broke out. That's how Pentecost begins—with little fires everywhere—just like Celeste Ng's book and the miniseries of the same name on HULU; Pentecost begins with little fires everywhere.

And like the readers of the book and watchers of the miniseries, many of us seeing the fires of Pentecost and present-day protests want to know what caused the fires. What did we miss? What were the warning signs?

Jesus Said Something is about to Happen

At first glance, those surprised by the fires may have missed the proverbial writing on the wall, or, literally, the title of the miniseries. One should not be surprised that a miniseries titled "Little Fires Everywhere" begins with a blazing fire. Similarly, one reading a book titled *Acts* should not be surprised that the book is replete with action. Jesus introduces and summarizes the actions of *Acts* saying to inquisitive disciples "It is not for you to know the times or the seasons which the Father has put under His own power, but you will receive power when the Holy Ghost comes upon you."These words serve as Jesus' forewarning that something was about to happen.

And when Jesus says something is going to happen, you can best believe it's going to happen. If Jesus says He is going do, you can believe that it will be done! If Jesus says Lazarus shall live, then instead of planning his funeral repast, get ready for his resurrection. If Jesus says the fish and loaves are enough to feed the crowd of over five thousand men, women, and children, and then make them sit down and start serving the meal. *Because the word of Jesus Christ the Son of God—the incarnation of God—is equal in power and authority to the word of God God's self.*

So Noah, if God says it's going to rain, forget the fact that the country is in the middle of a drought, get your hammer and start building an ark. Moses, if God says speak to Pharaoh, then take your stick and your s-s-s-s-stutter and get to talking. David, if God says He saw you, get the sackcloth and the ashes and repent of your sins. Hannah, if God says he heard your prayer, then start picking out the colors for the nursery. If God says, weeping endures for a night but joy comes in the morning, then keep the Kleenex in the bed with you but put the confetti and the noise makers on the night stand because in the morning, you're having a party.

If God says God will show up, don't look at the clock, just lay out the welcome mat for in due season, God will come and not tarry. If God, through Christ, says the Spirit of the Lord is upon me, to preach the good news to the poor, freedom for the prisoners, recovery of sight to the blind, set the captives free, and proclaim the year of the Lord's favor—then all of you racist and elitist gatekeepers of the status quo had better get ready because a revolution is coming.

Jesus told his disciples that power was coming. Jesus told them that the Holy Ghost was coming. Jesus told them that fire was coming. So when the Day of Pentecost was fully come in Acts 2,the little fire everywhere are merely a manifestation of what Jesus had already told them was coming.

For ten days, they had sequestered themselves in an upper room; waiting for what Jesus told them was coming. For ten days, they worked on filling voids in their leadership team, as they waited for what Jesus told them was coming. For ten days they prayed and prayed in anticipation of what they knew was coming. So when the Day of Pentecost had fully come, and they were all with one accord in one place, and suddenly they heard a sound from heaven, and little fires broke out everywhere, they didn't freak out because they knew this was coming.

And just like the darker-hued participants of this Pentecost pericope, who waited and waited, for years—and years, and years—disenfranchised darker-hued people in this country have been waiting: waiting for our American nightmare to end and authentic access to the American Dream to begin; waiting to be made whole after being broken by the system of slavery; waiting for fairness to come to the court system; waiting for good jobs and opportunities to come to the ghetto; waiting for economic equality; waiting for genuine justice. Waiting for real recognition; waiting for acknowledgement that we are the ones who built America's economy and institutions. Therefore, we are not surprised to look around America and see little fires everywhere; Jesus told us the fire was coming!

We Have Been Holding This in For Too Long

In "Little Fires Everywhere," as one learns more of the story behind the fire, it is no surprise that the Richards' house is set on fire because everyone in the house has something that they've been holding onto for too long. There are some secrets and some lies characters have been holding on to for too long. There are some truths and some troubles that everyone in the house had been holding onto for too long. Every character in the story has something they've been holding onto—history, hurts, habits, hang-ups. Every character plays the part of having it altogether on the outside but all of them are experiencing hell on the inside.

By the time the fire starts, then, it is easy to see how each character in the story contributed to the fire. It is also easy to see how the fire allows everybody to release some of what they have been holding. In like manner, the characters in the Pentecost narrative have been holding onto some things. They are men and women in the text who know that Jesus is alive. For 40 days they have seen him. They have walked with him and talked with him—but have had to keep the news to themselves.

On the 40th day, in Acts 1, they watch Jesus ascend to the heavens, but still they cannot tell anyone because instead of sending them out, Jesus told them to go   to an upper room and wait. So they wait—and hold it in—for one day, two days, three days, four days, five days, six days, seven days. They are still waiting—and holding it in—for eight days, nine days, ten whole days of waiting and holding it in. Acts 1:15 confirms that there were about 120 people in the room just waiting and holding it in. Today's text says they were all on one accord and they were all in the same place, and a fire broke out. Tongues sat upon each of them, and they began to speak as the Spirit—i.e. the fire—gave them ability. In other words, when the fire started, that which they had been holding in, they were finally able to let it out.

And in 2020, as fires burn from Washington, D.C. to Washington State, I submit that some folks who have been waiting and waiting and holding things in that are now being let out. Oppressed people have been holding their frustration in too long, and now that little fires are everywhere, they are finally letting their frustration out. Abused people have been holding their pain in too long. Overlooked people have kept their silence for too long. Unappreciated people have been holding their anger for too long. Displaced people have been holding their sense of forced instability for too long. Disrespected people have been holding on to the stain of being stigmatized for too long. African Americans have been holding on to the stigmas of others' stereotypes and chattel slavery for a long time. Native and Latin American people have been holding onto the injuries of their ancestral lands being stolen for a long time. Asian Americans have been holding onto the injuries of invisibility for too long. Racists have been holding on to the fear of their privileged positions being usurped. Now that little fires are burning everywhere, everyone is getting the opportunity to let all of their feelings and frustrations out.

Even you, the one reading these words, may be holding in feelings of anger, frustration, disappointment and defeat. Because in-person gatherings—including gatherings for worship—have been limited, perhaps you have been holding in acts of worship and praise. Because you haven't been able to gather in God's House, you've been holding in your "Hallelujah!" Your "Thank you Jesus!" Your dance! Your shout! But during this inaugural of Pentecost, the little fires everywhere are giving you an opportunity to let your praise out!

Fire Doesn't Care Who Gets Burned

On the Day of Pentecost, when the little fires everywhere erupted in the upper room, the text says they all were filled. Everyone who was present in the room was touched by the fires. The fires did not discriminate. The fires were not selective. The fires didn't favor some over others. Anyone and everyone in the vicinity of the fires were touched by their flames.

As little fires burn across the American landscape today, some may attempt to console themselves saying "they're not on my street or in my neighborhood." Today, there may not be any fires on your street or in your neighborhood, but as the fires continue to burn in neighboring cities, neighborhoods, and houses it is only a matter of time before the fire shows up in your neighborhood too. After all, fire is not a respecter of places, property, or people. It will burn who and whatever is in its path.

Hence you may be tempted to ignore the conditions that have caused these little fires everywhere. You can continue to ignore victims of racism, sexism, and Trump-ism. You can continue to ignore police brutality and the Black Lives Matter Movement. You can continue pretending the ills igniting these fires do not exist because they are not directly threatening you. However, if you play with the fire, by ignoring its presence, sooner or later, you, too, will get burned.

Something is about to combust

Acts 1:3-8 and 2:1-3

(The Message Translation)

Acts 1

3 After his suffering, he presented himself to them and gave many convincing proofs that he was alive. He appeared to them over a period of forty days and spoke about the kingdom of God.

4 On one occasion, while he was eating with them, he gave them this command: "Do not leave Jerusalem, but wait for the gift my Father promised, which you have heard me speak about.

5 For John baptized with water, but in a few days you will be baptized with the Holy Spirit."

6 Then they gathered around him and asked him, "Lord, are you at this time going to restore the kingdom to Israel?"

7 He said to them: "It is not for you to know the times or dates the Father has set by his own authority.

8 But you will receive power when the Holy Spirit comes on you; and you will be my witnesses in Jerusalem, and in all Judea and Samaria, and to the ends of the earth."

2:1 When the day of Pentecost came, they were all together in one place.

2 Suddenly a sound like the blowing of a violent wind came from heaven and filled the whole house where they were sitting.

3 They saw what seemed to be tongues of fire that separated and came to rest on each of them.

4 All of them were filled with the Holy Spirit and began to speak in other tongues[a] as the Spirit enabled them.

As we are both former English literature teachers, Dr Van Williams, pastor or Cedar Crest in Dallas of whom I share this collaborative series...and I had a discussion about the differences between the book and the series Little Fires Everywhere.. As we neared Pentecost, we shared the juxtaposition and commented on the "nice' parallel of the story line and the cultural/biblical connections with Pentecost ...and how in our houses we were to be little fires everywhere... then the protest escalated ... and it's a God moment...The original inspiration was....text, the film, But the prophetic message that has developed in real time is a right now relevant understanding that there are indeed little smoldering fires everywhere...the spiritual parallels are striking....

It is not mere coincidence in the timing of the shutdown and Pentecost weekend burning. Don't miss it ...there is a reason we are watching little fires everywhere...and it's cultural and political yes, but it's also spiritual... There is a sizzle... a rumbling of embers in the land, with an abundance of kindle...there is smoke that permeates the sky and a stench all too familiar...It has caused the reigniting of flames of resistance, and ignited a new blaze of enough is enough... the un-mattering of black lives is greater than the fear of death by Covid... greater than the fear of arrest ... it is steeped in history ... in systemic disregard..in the disdain of being the political ping pong ball for politicians...in being sick and tired of being sick and tired and it manifests as little fires everywhere... and when those little fire connect they become combustible! There is a Nigerian proverb that asserts, "The child that does not feel the warmth of the village. Will burn the village just to feel its warmth" ... There are little fires everywhere...

The text today is a familiar one...and though our norm is to commemorate what is called the birth of the church and to rejoice in the sanctification of the speaking in other tongues....to shout about how the glory filled the room and how the power fell on those in attendance, there is a back story...a history...a human struggle that precedes the supernatural. The disciples had just witnessed last words and ascension... they felt grief...uncertainty...Jesus was gone...headed to a room in pain...disciples like the community felt the pain loss. So they returned to the room, not only because they were obedient, but the truth is, like many of us... and like so many young African Americans, There was a mark on their heads...not always visible...but like Covid...looming...a pin and needles existence with a side of whose next?

At the point of our text, we join the disciples after the promise is given, but before its manifestation, before the arrival of the Holy Spirit. They are sequestered and apprehensive, and then something happens...and it changes everything. Something is about to combust...

How does this text line up with what's happening today...Here's the set up : Monday was Memorial Day I decided to barbeque...I hadn't lit a fire on a pit in years, and little did I know that my process would serve as an object lesson, as an analogous paradigm for this message. To cook food on the grill combustion is required, but it involves processes internal and external... It requires anticipation, alignment, an accelerant, and a lighting action... It's Pentecost, and in the world, and prayerfully in the church, there are little fires everywhere! And something is getting ready to combust!

Anticipation of the promise

The disciples are in anticipation of the promise...Jesus said go and wait...but he didn't give a timeline...Leaders say, Playing by the rules, go to school, be a good citizen, do the right things and things will change. Yet more persons die in the streets at the hand of those who vow to protect and serve. There is a constant state of fear from mothers and fathers...who's next? Like the disciples, the prospect of untimely death hovers. Then the frustration comes ... how long? Do I stay the course or try a different route? We cry how long...The disciples asked the Lord "When will your kingdom come?" We ask "When will they stop killing us?" When will we receive the promise? We have been waiting, but when *will* we be judged by the content of our character not by the color of our skin. In the watershed poem written by Langston Hughes, Harlem, Hughes chronicles the stages of dreams that are delayed, asking "what happens to a dream deferred?"Dr Martin Luther King declared however, we can't wait! The frustration is generationally diverse but requires being open to instruction...but it must be mutual instruction...Moses had the rod...but Joshua's infiltration facilitated a Promised Land arrival.

Jesus said stay...wait. There is process; there is purpose. We must get ready to complete preparation and choose leadership. We must get ready for what's on the way. They had to arrive at a common purpose - a common process...

There are little fires everywhere, and they are not new. The disciples in that room faced uncertainty. They had marks on their head, but they were anticipating the promise... anticipating something greater. They didn't know the means or the timing, but they knew it was coming!

Little fires are everywhere. Something is getting ready to combust

Alignment is imperative

There was anticipation, but there has to be alignment. Alignment for the disciples meant in one place, of same mind with unity of heart. For disciples it was same location. However, for those who are in this time, alignment is not a municipality, but it is same mindset; not same street but the same sentiment. It is not having the same story, but having your back...little fires are everywhere....The Alignment is multiracial; it is not monolithic.

There was a picture taken in Louisville of several Caucasian women standing between the police and protesters, the words on the poster they held stated: "this is what you do with your privilege." They aligned with the principles and the people. There is power in alignment....

Here is an illustration:

When I began the set up for the barbeque, I socially distanced the coals because I thought the spreading of the coals would make the fire cover more area...they were lit but alone...the first ones I used were also older and were not as flammable, so I went to the dollar store, and though not a premium brand, these coals were new and fresh. I didn't take out the old ones, but lined them in a pyramid, and lit them together. They were aligned well to receive the heat from the others. They were in the right place together...and in formation.

The disciples and the protests this weekend were in the same place, one physically and spiritually. They were like minded and connected, not socially distanced in heart. They were ready to walk in their purpose and to complete their mission!

Something is about to combust!

Accelerant makes the difference

While being on one accord is important...there is still a need for an accelerant, for fires to combust. For the barbeque, the accelerant is lighter fluid on coals. The disciples and protesters were in one place and in alignment...but on one accord is what readies us, but is not enough to light, to combust...to blaze! We live a tale of two cities (classes), the haves and the have not's...privilege and poverty, and the statistics are mind boggling. Being on one accord is so powerful because it requires intentionality. I don't have to walked in your shoes to empathize with your walk...I don't have to look like you to respect you as a person ...I don't have to be homeless...to see you ...We don't have to be the same to share common care...when we share

Common purpose, common process, common perspective, and common push for change is the accelerant that positions us for the promise...both politically and spiritually. When we are on one accord and establish common purpose, process, perspective and push for change, the church will harness the power of the Holy Spirit...the accelerant will ready little fires everywhere! Something is about to combust!!!

Action: Light the Match

In the upper room the Spirit arrived violently...it wasn't a Quiet storm...but mighty rushing wind. It caused a commotion; it made people run to see what was happening. It started with wind, and the wind brought the cloven tongues of little fires everywhere... In the novel, the fires were set in rooms, in small places, burning in close proximity. The same happened with the protests. Don't you know fire doesn't care, and when you start a fire...fire draws fire and the result is combustible....Church, we have watched what happens when anticipation, alignment, and accelerant are lit by one match of too much. "No more" from Minnesota to Denver from Louisville to La because of not just George Floyd and Breonna Taylor, but far too many names igniting multiple fires that caused combustion! *What happens church when we walk in anticipation; align ourselves in one place and the harness the accelerant of one accord all.* It takes is one match...one light to start little fires everywhere...Pentecost fires everywhere....fires of boldness, fires of stand for and for truth...fires of change, fires of hope , fires that speak up, are prayed up...then get up, fires that participate, fires that show the church being the church.

There is a story of a man who did not go to church.... He was not interested in church...and there was only one in the area. It was cold and dead—a social club, - No heart for the community...no care for the downtrodden, the hurting, or the marginalized... One day the church building caught on fire, and the whole town ran toward it to help extinguish the flames...including the man who didn't go to church....Someone hollered out: "Hey, this is something new for you, the first time we've ever seen you running to church!" He replied, "This is the first time I've ever seen the church on fire!

Church, it's Pentecost. We must bring the fire ...Jeremiah said the power of God was like fire shut up in his bones. Where is your fire? We must be little fires everywhere, yes Holy Spirit filled, but we must also be lit for community...a lit for justice... lit for the needs of others....that's when we reflect the one who is the light...that's when we together can cause a blaze that will set the world on fire...We must be Matt. 25 and set fires for the least of these. When you saw me naked clothed me...little fire...when you saw me in prison...and came to see about me and fought for me...little fire...when you saw me sick...and your vote helped me get food health care...little fire...when you fed me...and made sure I could keep eating...little fire...when you mourned with me, protected me, when you stood with me...little fire..Our fires together everywhere will cause combustion...and the power of the Lord will

turn things around...and justice will come...and souls will be saved...
Something is about to combust...are you here for it!!!?? Can you
declare spirit of the living God fall fresh on me...?

Song: Spirit of the Living God

Fall afresh on me

Melt me,

Mold me,

Fill me,

Use me

Spirit of the Living God

Fall afresh on me

Daniel Iverson

First Sunday After Pentecost

Let it Burn

Divided tongues, as of fire, appeared among them,
And a tongue rested on each of them.
Acts 2:3

At some point in life, all of us learn that we are not in control. Some learn this lesson in menial ways like planning a birthday party or other celebratory gathering, when nothing goes according to plan. Others learn the lesson through a major life-change event like being served divorce papers by the one to whom you pledged "till death do us part." Others perhaps are learning this lesson presently as the resolutions and goals you set for 2020 are being upended since theCOVID-19 pandemic arrived and practically shut everything down. If, by chance, you have not yet learned that you are not in control, just keep living and I guarantee that the day will come when you will realize that you are not in control.

You may be the "man" or even the "husband" but you are not in control. You may be the "manager" or the "Mrs." but you are not in control. You think the titles in front of your name mean you are in control? You think the alphabets after your name mean you are in control? You think because you are the head of a household or chief cook and bottle washer you are in control? You think because you are the parent, or the Pastor or the President—you think that means you are in control? No, no, no dear friend! Your title may make you feel like you are in charge, but make no mistake, your title does not mean you are in control.

In Charge versus In Control

To be in charge means to be responsible for. To be in control means to possess an ability to direct. To be in charge means to hold the title. To be in control means to have ultimate authority. So understand that even if your title says you are in charge that does not mean you are in control.

Someone needs to tell that both to the talking head on television and to Donald Trump in the White House. Because as little fires have broken out everywhere around the country—fires of anger, fires of protest, fires of riots, and even fires of vandalism and looting—as fires calling for justice, calling for reform, calling for an end to police brutality, systematic racism, and white privilege—as little fires have broken out everywhere, the talking heads on television are saying somebody needs to get this under control, and Trump is talking like he is in control. Some state governors have mobilized their National Guards, but they are not in control. Trump has threatened to send in the United States military to "restore law and order" but neither he nor they are in control.

We know they are not in control because there have been people protesting for 12 straight days. We know they are not in control because this past week, as we saw video after video of law enforcement officials pushing protesters, the protesters were pushing right back. We know they are not in control, because even as police were firing canisters of tear gas to disperse the crowds, the crowds just kept coming. We know they are not in control, because when protesters showed up outside the White House, Donald Trump turned off all the lights and retreated to its underground bunker.

We know they are not in control, because even while the Corona virus pandemic is still running rampant, it is not just American protesters putting themselves at risk, but people in Britain, Australia, Italy, Germany, another countries have been putting themselves at greater risk for contracting corona virus to protest the racial injustice they see happening here, and in their own countries as well. So as much as people with titles talk about control, and act like they're in control, they are not in control.

Control or at least the semblance of being in control is a major motif that we also see in Celeste Ng's "Little Fires Everywhere."The two main matriarchs—Mia and Elena—work tirelessly to be in control. Mia moves her and her daughter all across the country trying to be in control. Elena does not want to birth a fourth child because she's trying to be in control. Throughout the miniseries, they are trying to control their children, trying to control their lives, trying to control their reputations, their narratives, what people think, and what people say. The children, like their parents, are also trying to be in control—in control of their secrets, their lives, their feelings and their failures. Yet no matter how hard everyone works to maintain control, the little fires set at the end of the miniseries is evidence that none of them are in control. Physically, socially, emotionally, and—yes—even spiritually—none of them are in control.

The same can be said about the little fires everywhere in Acts 2. As the fires are burning, no one is in control. The followers of Jesus have been meeting and praying for 10 days, but none of them are in control. They have held elections to fill the void in their leadership   team, but none of them are in control. They were in one place and on one accord, but none of them were in control.

Who *Is* In Control?

The reason none of them were in control, and the reason why none of us are in control, and the reason why neither Trump, nor the military, nor racists, nor anybody else is in control is because God is in control.

The text says "They heard a sound from heaven"—that's God being in control. The sound filled the house where they were sitting—that's God being in control. There appeared tongues of fire which sat on each of them—that's God being in control. They began to speak in different languages as the Spirit gave them utterance—that's God being in control. The people in the room were parties to what was happening, but they weren't in control of what was happening. They were participants in what was happening but they weren't in control of what was happening. As humans, we can be instruments, we can be vessels, we can be conduits, we can be carriers, we can be parties of, or participants in, but ultimately, God is the One in control.

They're Trying to Stop the Fire

In the text, although God is in control of the fires that are burning, and although God is present in the fires that are burning, others arrive in the room trying to extinguish the fires. Acts 2:5 says there were devout Jews dwelling in Jerusalem who were from every nation under the heaven. And when the sound occurred, they all came together and were confused, because they heard Galileans speaking in the various languages of the lands from whence they had come. Some of the confused people asked each other "Whatever could this mean?" Others made fun of the scene saying the followers of Jesus were drunk and full of new wine.

Please note the attendance and attitude of those who arrived in the room after they heard the sound. None of them were invited. None of them were on the guest list. They simply saw what was happening and showed up either to instigate or to insult. They showed up to question or to criticize. They showed up to talk about what was happening to everyone else when they, the arriving spectators, needed help themselves.

The spectators' attendance and attitude is akin to the effect of broke people giving you financial advice; or habitually unemployed people giving you career advice; thrice married, thrice divorced people giving you marital advice; or oppressors trying to give oppressed people advice. While they call themselves trying to help *you*, they really need someone to help them!

That was an issue in "Little Fires Everywhere," the parents and people in positions of power were always trying to give advice when they oftentimes were the ones most in need of advice. In the context of current events, people who want to tell you how to protest are trying to put out the fire. People, who want to minimize the purpose of these protests as if they are just tantrums, are trying to put out the fire. People, who want to make fun of it or ignore it, as if it will soon go away, are trying to put out the fire. However, I have come today to say that whatever, God has sparked in you, let it burn! The fire God has placed inside of you, let them burn. The fires of truth that God is bringing out of you, let them burn.

Our learning means nothing without God's burning!

People of African descent in America have played by the rules far too long. We have gone to school, and gotten jobs, and been model citizens. We have protested injustice but, as a people, still not prospered. We have marched but still haven't made it. We have hollered but still haven't been heard. We have complained but are still being unfairly and unjustly killed and incarcerated. And since none of these measures have worked, we've had to comingle our social learning with Diving burning.

The burning is what allows you to do what people say you can't do. The burning is what allows you to go where people say you can't go. The burning is what allows you to have what people say you can't have. It's not your learning, it's God's burning. It's not your knowledge, it's God's fire. It's not your know-how, it's God's anyhow. It's not your know-how, it's God's somehow. Because somehow, God can bless you anyhow, even when you don't have the know-how!

If you do not believe that consider the named followers of Christ who are present in the Pentecost narrative. Peter, Andrew, James, and John were fishermen, businessmen, and entrepreneurs—they had learning. Matthew was good at math and worked for the government as a tax collector—he had learning. Simon the Zealot was active in the world of politics and social affairs—he had learning. Phillip was a follower of John the Baptist, who left John when he met Jesus—he had learning. Nathanael was the first person to call Jesus the Son of God and King of Israel. Thaddeus wanted to know all he could about God. James was short in size but big in faith. Thomas would not believe Christ had risen until he had irrefutable evidence. All of them had walked and talked with Jesus for 3 years—they had learning.

They knew about the systems of the world. They knew about social order. They knew how religion could sometimes be influenced by racist politics (and vice versa).They knew how to survive and how to make a living by operating in the world's economy. And they also knew who Jesus was—not the Romanized, white Jesus, but the real Jesus—the darker skinned Jesus who was their friend. Yet for all of their learning, they are still an oppressed people who had not experienced the burning.

Listen, you may have learned to recite "one nation under God with liberty and justice for all." You may have learned to sing "God bless America." Yet all that you have learned never came to life without some burning. American independence did not come peacefully, it, literally, came through some burning. It came through non-peaceful protests like the Boston Tea Party. It came through little fires everywhere like the Revolutionary War. It came because people were frustrated learning about the promises of government but never experiencing the protection of that government. And in their frustration, they took their learning and merged it with burning.

Some Black church people would describe it this way: you may have learned how to pray, but your prayers lose their potency without the burning. You may have learned how to sing, but your song loses its strength without the burning. You may have learned how to preach, but your preaching loses it power without the burning. You may have learned about faith, but faith cannot function without a burning. Because it's not about what you know is your head, it's about who you know in your heart.

That's why Jesus told the disciples wait, until you receive the promise of the Father. Wait until you receive power from on high. Wait until you hear a sound from heaven that speaks to your very souls. Wait until the fire falls. Because it's not by your power, nor by your might, but by My Spirit says the Lord. My Spirit will give you life. My Spirit will give you strength. My Spirit will give you guidance. My Spirit will give you direction. My Spirit will give you comfort. Whatever you need, God says My Spirit will give.

The People You Are Trying to Leave out, God is Working to Let In

The very people some make fun of are the very ones God is trying to move through! The very ones some laugh at, are the ones being used by the Lord. In the text the followers of Christ have been empowered by the fires of the Holy Ghost to speak in the various languages of the world. They are talking and testifying about what God has done and what God is doing to usher in God's kingdom. They are worshipping God in the midst of the fires.

Then some religious people—the scripture calls them devout men, so, religious people—came in critiquing the worship and work of those who were recipients of Diving burning. Religious people critiqued what was right and what was wrong about their worship and their work—what they liked and what they didn't like what they found acceptable and what they found unacceptable. You know how it is: everybody wants to put their own rules on the way you express yourself. Everybody wants to put their own words into the way you witness and the way you work. They tell you that you're not doing it the right way because you're not doing it their way. They accuse you of doing the wrong thing because you're not doing their thing.

That was the critique that these commentators brought to the Upper Room on the Day of Pentecost. They were saying that what was happening in the house couldn't be real because it wasn't the way things used to be. So they made fun of the people who were speaking in different tongues. They called the people drunk who were celebrating being delivered.

Yet I sagaciously suggest that the means of expressing themselves that the spectators called wrong, God is calling right. The practices they want to put out, God is trying to bring in. The very thing they don't understand is the same thing God is trying to encourage.

And Peter tells the people this is what God spoke to us through the prophet Joel: "That in the last days, I will pour out my Spirit on all flesh"—not just the flesh that you think is worthy of it. And when that happens, God says the sons whom your arrogance says are weak, and the daughters whom your misogyny says are dumb, are the very people I will use to prophesy. Your young men whom you have written off as mere workers, God says I will give them visions. And your old men whom you think can't do anything; God says I will give them dreams. And the ones who carry the title "servant" I will fill them with My Spirit! Because the very people you try to leave out, are the very ones whom God is trying to let in!

You may not like the way people are protesting. You may not like the way people are expressing their frustration. You may not even like that the conditions they are protesting are the reality of this country. Yet whether you like or dislike, agree or disagree, the people you are trying to leave out, God is trying to pull them in!

The burning is the blessing that leads to the breakthrough

There were those who could not understand why Jesus followers had locked themselves away and began having a prayer summit that lasted for 10 days. There were those who did not understand what it meant on the 10th day when they heard a sound from heaven, saw the tongues of fire, and heard the gospel being preached in their own language. Acts 2:12 says that onlookers began to gather and ask each other "What does this mean?" And others began to mock and make fun of them saying "These men are full of new wine." But Peter stood up saying "These men are not drunk. They are filled with the Spirit of God." The onlookers came trying to put the fire out, but Peter began preaching in order to keep the fire going.

The episode of Peter's preaching in Acts 2 reminds me of a call and response chant that I used to hear at house parties and college parties as I was coming of age. The DJ would get on the microphone and say "the roof...the roof is on fire." And the crowd would respond "We don't need no water, let the __________ burn." The fire is our purpose for being here. The fire suggests that we have succeeded in our celebrating.

In other words, the fire was not to incite fear, it was a celebration of faithfulness. The followers of Jesus were faithful to Jesus' instructions, and God was faithful to God's promise of giving Jesus' followers power. If then there is a calling or conviction on your life, remain faithful to it. If there is a godly cause you support, stay faithful to it. If there is a wrong you seek right, an injustice you seek to overturn, an ill you desire to heal, remain faithful to attaining and achieving it. You may not always feel like doing the work but remain faithful anyway. In God's time and in God's way, God will send God's fire.

Purpose in the Flames

Acts 2:3-8, 12

Then, what looked like flames or tongues of fire appeared and settled on each of them.

4 And everyone present was filled with the Holy Spirit and began speaking in other languages, [b] as the Holy Spirit gave them this ability.

5 At that time there were devout Jews from every nation living in Jerusalem.

6 When they heard the loud noise, everyone came running, and they were bewildered to hear their own languages being spoken by the believers.

7 They were completely amazed. "How can this be?" they exclaimed. "These people are all from Galilee, 8 and yet we hear them speaking in our own native languages!

12 They stood there amazed and perplexed. "What can this mean?" they asked each other.

As we continue in our series Little Fires Everywhere, reignited for revival...it is necessary to return to the literary text for some connected perspective. The lives of the persons in the book and series are plagued with inconsistencies and secrets, unclear and filled with the facade of expectation. When those are the conditions of life, when truth is hidden and crusted over for an extended period of time the climate is ripe for conflict. One of the mothers in the story often manipulates the environment to maintain a false sense of normalcy, while the other manipulates it with a sense of boldness that is but a defense mechanism for the fear that infiltrates her psyche. Eventually, the rug will be pulled, the sheet will be uncovered and we are left with the prevailing question...what's going on? Or to be in keeping with the text...What does it mean? How will their ways impact their children and families? The search for fake peace in this time is much like these mothers in "*Little Fires Everywhere*". There are those who want it to feel peaceful, though the rumbling crackling of fire has been building for decades. There are many all over the land right now asking this very question because there was no awareness of the depth of the issues, no thought beyond their own expectations, and pseudo (fake) vision of an American Dream (that was a always a hologram) in the midst of a ego feeding nightmare, The status quo had and has had no desire to know more than can be ingested in small bites...life as a buffet of horderves, with no capacity to handle the rich truth of the entree...So many are looking at the times, the situation, and they have been taught to say the right things, but there is no grand evidence that they get it...much like some of us who know the churchy catch phrases...but our hearts are still in need of transformation.

As we continue to navigate through Covid 19 and the fire of protest continues to burn in cities across the country, and in the world...there is a message in the Pentecostal inquisition by those who saw, heard, felt and listened to that which they had failed to expect to see, hear, feel or listen to. ...and it left them, and the move of the many today with a need to understand the purpose in the fire!

There is so much evidence that persons are clueless just as they had no idea what God was doing at Pentecost, there is a lack of understanding as to how God is using this time, this season, these happenings to send a message to the world, to political systems and to the church...The church particularly cannot not afford to be absent, impotent and invisible in this time…This time is crudicle, (a word mistakenly coined by a former student who wrote the word in an essay as a cross between crucial and critical...)for if we are not conscious of the gravity, the absence and silence of the true church reduces the word of God to a prop...

The Word of God can not be a tool used for frivolous photo ops and age old proof text and to enable and uphold the oppressive use of religion. Nor can church people remain in silence and subsequently condone tear gas and rubber bullets to remove the unseen, unimportant and the "in the way". It cannot afford to fail to view the sacred text in collaboration...as the Wesley Theological Seminary webinar I watched this week on Embracing the Text declared...Sacred texts are best understood in community! We must never forget that the world is watching the church... not the buildings... but the church... We must not in the midst of our way maker praise fail to remember that as liberator Jesus...his death on the cross (we commemorated a few moments ago) was not only liberation for our soul into salvation, but of our lives as agents for justice...Jesus lived as both fully human and divine and he didn't operate in them separately...his humanity and is divinity were a homeostatic union... The work of justice is the work of the Christ's church... In order to be catalysts for understanding and clarity, we must seek the purpose in the fires...and in all our getting...get an understanding... (That's wisdom) There is purpose in the flames

In that room so long ago... a movement occurred, but those outside were drawn to the spectacle... drawn to the happening ... drawn to the smoke...ready to give commentary... but unprepared to listen to the Crackling of the fires...the hovering of the fires on their heads...

There is a need to understand the power of fire as destructive yes...but as purifier...it is no less volatile as purifier but the purpose is different.... it is also an Illuminator. The intention of the symbol was to show them that the Holy Spirit would illuminate them, as fire gives light. "He shall lead you into all truth (John 16:13). But fire doth more than give light: it inflames; and the flames which sat upon each showed them that they were to be ablaze with love, intense with zeal, burning with self-sacrifice; and that they were to go forth among men to speak not with the chill tongue of deliberate logic, but with burning tongues of passionate pleading; persuading and entreating men to come unto Christ that they might live. The fire signified inspiration. God was about to make them speak under a divine influence, to speak as the Spirit of God should give them utterance.

There is purpose in the flames!

Purpose in the Sounding -

The sound shifts the focus...there is a sound in the room and in the street... a voice, a chant which suggests that listening is imperative...Do we hear the wind...Do we hear the pain the struggle...Do we hear the cries, the experiences and the trauma...Holy Spirit shifts the atmosphere...can you hear the sound!!! Are we listening! In James Cone's and Gayraud S Wilmore's anthology of theological thought Black Theology: a documentary history, Joseph A Johnson Jr., in his article Jesus the Liberator quotes Professor Ernst Fuch who calls the rise of the gospel a "speech event"...and the early church as a "language phenomenon"...yes the sound of the rushing wind was attention getting, but the outpouring of language of dialectic left those who heard with a desire to understand and empowered those speaking to be heard. The sound of pain, angst, frustration, of no more, of enough is enough is being heard and spoken not in America only but in Africa, Europe, Australia...same message in tongues each can understand. Are we listening?

The work of the Holy Spirit is not silent...for faith cometh by hearing. Charles Spurgeon reminds us that as God gave us ears...God must have intended us to hear something, and as we have tongues he must have meant us to speak. There is a sound and we must listen...As Howard Thurman declared...Give me the listening ear...eyes that are willing to see! There is purpose in the flames...

Purpose in the Speaking -

The content of the speaking embodies the meaning. The phenomenon was the beginning...the attention getter, but the challenge is do the words move us? Can we hear the voices and not dismiss them? The question is asked "What does this mean?" We heard the words...but what is the meaning...what is the comprehension? It is not enough to understand the decoding of a language, if we lack the capacity to comprehend its meaning. At its core, the message of this uprising, the little fires that are everywhere, is not merely hash tags. They embody more than #wecantbreathe #blacklivesmatter #Colorofchange...but what is the meaning, what is the depth of the purpose? Those at Pentecost were speaking in native language and were understood but not comprehended...the lack of clear understanding is the disconnect when we are hearers of the word but not doers...comprehension compels change...it is as if the words black lives matter came out last week, but the movement has been speaking since 2013! Almost seven years of dismissal Seven years were spent hearing but not comprehending truth. How many lives could have been saved in seven years if their lives had mattered before George Floyd...Mr. Floyd's real life murder in a virtual space with folks home and on social media, opened ears, opened eyes, and opened hearts. There is a purpose in speaking verbally, written, in protest, in defiance. Jesus said you shall receive power after the Holy Ghost comes. The power of the Holy Spirit opened their mouths to speak with a clarity that caused folk to listen...that same power is available to us today...There is purpose in the flame!

Purpose in the Stand-

Peter -has always been rambunctious...but his boldness magnifies with the Spirit, and he harnesses the power and stands. He stands up, speaks up and in turn the naysayers shut up! For there are always three types of persons who receive the message...those who get it because they are open...those who reject even though they understand...and those who because they lack understanding or concern decide to minimize the importance of what is heard. Peter is not passive when he hears their response; he meets them with warrior like boldness. Whether it is Covid 19 and the lack of respect for the disease or those who wish the protest would just go away...Boldness is necessary...There is no option in this season. As the early church was a movement to build the kingdom, the church must be involved and bold when it comes to justice. This is Jesus work and there is no place for weak Christians. Don't wear the name if you can't represent! This is not the time for the faint at heart. We must be on the battlefield for the Lord and serve in the ways that show that we warriors for Justice. If only your hallelujah belongs to God and you have no heart for the people...you aint ready!

If your thank you Jesus can't shift to a war cry...you aint ready

If your victory shout is quiet in the midst of the struggle...you aint ready

If your privilege is more important than your service...you aint ready

If your silence speaks louder than your voice....you definitely aint ready...

The spirit of God came and is here to give us 'stand up' power...not sideline power ...not stay back power ...not shake your head power...the spirit gives power to stand in ... stand up... stand with... and stand against ...this is not a spectator sport. Kingdom work requires those filled with the spirit and justice work demands those who understand the purpose in the flame.

HOUSE FIRE AND MARSHMALLOWS (Illustration)

There is a story of a family having a barbecue, but when a crisis comes, they show up, but they are unprepared to be of assistance. "We were visiting our neighbors and having a family barbeque. As the coals from our barbecue burned down, our hosts passed out marshmallows and long roasting forks. Just then, two fire trucks roared by, sirens blaring, and lights flashing. They stopped at a house right down the block. All twelve of us raced out of the back yard, down the street, where we found the owners of the blazing house standing by helplessly. They glared at us with looks of disgust. Suddenly, we realized why...we were all still holding our roasting forks with marshmallows on them.

We have run to the fires... they are burning everywhere... but what's in our hands...tools to help or marshmallows on a fork...what's in our hands...the gifts we have, our skill set, our abilities, our hearts...or are we just watching from a distance hoping it's soon over so things can get back to the comfortable or the fake. There is purpose in the flames and we need Holy Spirit illumination to rain down on us….we need the power to fall on us... so the sound we make will cause righteous commotion, the words we speak will be heard and the stand we take with change hearts...there is purpose in the flame...let your power fall Lord...let it fall...till we catch on fire...till we are little fires everywhere...till we think right...do right..live right... love right... and until justice rolls down like a mighty stream...let your power fall!

Song of Decision: Holy Spirit, Richard Smallwood

Holy Spirit fall fresh on me,
Lord, anoint us; we yield our all to thee;
For we know that yokes are broken,
And the captives are set free;
So let it fall down
Fall down,

Fall down on me
We need the power of the Holy Spirit, Holy Spirit
Send your anointing, let it fall down
Fall down,
Fall down on me

Second Sunday After Pentecost

Ownership Has Its Privileges

All of them were filled with the Holy Spirit.
Acts 2:4a

Anyone who has seen the miniseries "Little Fires Everywhere" focuses attention on the storylines of Mia and Elena. This is obviously justified as they are the persons occupying the spotlight or primary roles. The story centers on their families, their children, their parents, their messes, their mistakes. However, there is another character, which I believe truly holds the story together and makes it "work"—Bebe Chow.

Bebe is a Chinese immigrant who works with Mia at the Chinese restaurant. In the course of a conversation, Mia learns that Bebe gave birth to a daughter. Suffering through an episode of post-partum depression, when she is unable to buy formula for her baby because she is70 cents short, Bebe leaves her infant daughter at a fire station. In a separate conversation that Mia has with Elena, she learns that Elena's White friends are in the final process of adopting a Chinese baby who was abandoned at a local fire station. Putting two and two together, Mia suspects that the Chinese baby that Elena's White friends have named Mirabelle is the baby that Bebe gave birth to and had named May Ling Chow.

Bebe has been depressed ever since she left her baby at that fire station. Bebe has been wondering about and looking for her baby ever since she left her at that fire station. And when Mia tells her that she thinks her baby—MayLing—is the baby Elena's friends have renamed Mirabelle—and are trying to permanently adopt her—there is nothing and nobody who can stop Bebe from possessing—or taking ownership of taking ownership of—her baby.

Bebe bursts into the McCullough's house as they are having a birthday party for the baby to confirm that the baby they are calling

Mirabelle is really her baby. Bebe tries to take the baby because she is convinced that it is her baby. Bebe and the McCullough's go to court to legally determine parentage and guardianship of the baby. And while it is acknowledged that Bebe is the baby's biological mother, the court determines that the McCullough's are the baby's lawful parents.

And while I do not want to give away the ending, let me simply say that Bebe does not care what Elena says, or the McCullough's say, or what the courts say. Bebe never gives up in her quest to possess that which she has produced. She insists over and over again, "this is my baby. This is my child. It does not matter what has happened since her birth date and this date—because I made her she is mine. And I won't let anything or anybody keep me from what is mine."

We Belong to God

In her pertinacity to possess what she has produced—her steadfast single-mindedness to be with the baby she birthed—Bebe serves as an embodiment of God's love for God's children. Although sin separated us, God declares "I will do whatever it takes just to have you."Physically, you are mine because I made you in my image. Spiritually, you are mine because I blew my essence into you to give you life. I will fight the Devil himself so I can have you. I will invoke the law so I can have you. I'll send my only begotten Son to save you from sin so I can have you. I'll send my Spirit to seal you and strengthen you so I can have you.

God (like Bebe) embodies the lyrics of Smokey Robinson: "Ain't no mountain high enough, Ain't no valley low enough, Ain't no river wide enough to keep me from getting to you."And that is what we are witnessing on the Day of Pentecost   in Acts 2.We are witnessing God claiming what God created, God occupying what God already owns, and God possessing that which God has produced. For the Holy Ghost—for all that we understand it to be—symbolize God's ownership. It symbolizes God's acceptance—and acceptance is mutual.

Acceptance is Mutual

Both parties have to accept its conditions for a contract to be valid. Both parties have to accept the vows for a marriage to be valid. Both parties have to accept its terms for an agreement tube made or be valid. So while you may be happy and proud to proclaim that you have accepted God, the other question is has God accepted you?

This is some good Wesleyan theology. For John Wesley would have us understand that the gift of salvation is the First Blessing, but the gift of the Holy Ghost is the Second Blessing. Confessing Christ is the first blessing, but having Him confess you are the Second Blessing. Salvation maybe your initiation, but the indwelling of the Holy Ghost is God's confirmation of your initiation. And God is saying to us that some of us are claiming initiation—and operating in initiation—but haven't received any confirmation. Again, because it's not just about have you confessed and accepted God, but has God gifted you with the Holy Ghost to confirm God's acceptance of you? Acceptance is mutual.

That's why protests are still happening in the streets because Senate Majority Leader Mitch McConnell may say that America made up for enslaving Africans when Barak Obama was elected President—but Black folks aren't accepting it. America may say that we are land of the free, but oppressed minorities and women are not accepting it. Police cars may say "to serve and protect"—but people who have seen law enforcement officers slaughter and pillage are not accepting it.

We are not accepting it when just this past Friday another Black man, in Atlanta was killed while running away from cops after being caught sleeping in the drive-thru at Wendy's. We are not accepting it when the police officers have still not been charged in the death of Breonna Taylor, and the recently released police report does not document that it was the police who killed her. We are not accepting it when Candace Owens brings up George Floyd's run-ins with the law as if that excuses his murder by law enforcement officials. We are not accepting it because the whole world is calling for change. The whole world is calling for justice. The whole world is calling for an end to White privilege, racism, and other inequities.

And the whole world is calling for it because we recognize that ownership has its privileges.

Government leaders don't own all the power, the people who vote in local and federal elections are the ones who really own the power. The military does not own the American flag—every person who lives in this country owns that flag. You don't own this country—every citizen who lives in this country owns this country. The psalmist reminds us that the earth is the Lord's and the fullness thereof—the world and they that dwell therein. And because we own it, we can protest to protect it. Because we own it, we can burn it to make it better. Because we own it, you can't tell us to love it the way it is or leave it altogether. Because we own it, ownership has its privileges.

In the text, the followers of Christ were being owned by God in that upper room. And while they were exhibiting the fruits of their ownership, spectators showed up and tried to shut them down. They talked about them trying to shut them down. They criticized them trying to shut them down. They laughed at them trying to shut them down. But what the spectators who tried to shut it down did not realize is that ownership has its privileges. When you know who you are and whose you are it has its privileges. When you know who you belong to and who and what belongs to you, it has its privileges.

Ownership changes in the content of your conversation.

For the text says that when people from every nation under the heavens came to the place where they heard the sound from heaven that they found the followers of Christ—who were all Jews—speaking the languages of every nation under the heavens. When they came, they heard native Hebrew speakers speaking the language of the Cappadocians, Phrygians, and Pamphylians. They heard native Hebrew speakers speaking the languages of Egypt, Libya, and Italy. They heard native Hebrew speakers speaking the language of Cretans and Arabs.

But just as significant as *that* they were speaking is *what* they were speaking. Because the text says they weren't just having a common conversation but Acts 2:11 says they were talking about "the wonderful works of God."In every language under the heaven, they were conversing about "the wonderful works of God."In languages that they had never learned they were conversing about "the wonderful works of God."

These are the same people who were talking about earthly authority in Acts 1. Now they're talking about God's abundance in Acts 2.These are the same people who were worried about position in Acts 1. Now they're speaking of God being worthy of the praise in Acts 2.These are the same people who were dialoging about what they would do in Acts 1. Now they are dialoguing about what God is doing in Acts 2.Because when you understand your ownership, the content of your conversation changes too.

You go from talking about "woe is me," to talking about "worthy is the Lamb."You go from talking about how you don't have enough, to about how God supplies more than enough. You go from talking about the problem and start talking about the Problem Solver. You go from talking about what they did to you to talking about what God is doing through you. I can't talk like I used to talk, because I'm not in that place anymore. I'm not down anymore. I'm not depressed anymore. I'm not defeated anymore. I'm not desperate anymore.

So if you call me, thinking you're going to get another participant in your pity party, you called the wrong person. If you came by to converse about the hopelessness of your crisis, you came by the wrong house. If you want to go out so we can complain about all the hell that we are going through, then you need to invite somebody else. I don't have those conversations anymore. I don't have those pity parties anymore. I don't feel hopeless and helpless anymore. That season of is over.

So now I have a new way of talking! Now I talk like the head and not the tail. Now I talk like I'm above and not beneath. Now I talk like I'm a child of the King! Now I talk like I have the victory! Now I talk like God is for me! And if you hang around me long enough, and let me talk to you long enough, you're going to start talking like me too!!!Because ownership changes the content of your conversation!

Ownership changes the power of your proclamation.

The text says that while the followers of Christ were having this conversation, some of the spectators accused them of being drunk. That's what the text says, it says that some of the spectators who showed up because they heard the sound mocked them—or made fun of them—saying they were full of cheap new wine. Then, verse 14 says that Peter stood up with the other 11 and *raised his voice.* Don't miss that—it's small but it's saying something. There was a conversation going on, but when some of the spectators started to make fun of what was happening, Peter and the other eleven stood up adepter *raised his voice…*

And you know how it is when you are having what you think is a good conversation and then somebody raises their voice. All of a sudden the conversation is over. All of a sudden the atmosphere is changed. All of a sudden, everybody else, who was in the vicinity, having their own conversation shut up, so they can hear what's going on — because somebody, raised their voice.

That's what's happening in the text. At first it was just conversation. But when some of the spectators started laughing and making fun of the conversation—Peter raises his voice and the conversation turns into a proclamation. As they were conversing, it was a private dialogue, but when Peter raised his voice it turned into a public declaration. No longer were people listening and responding to the wondrous works of God in their various languages, but everybody turned to hear what Peter was saying   in   his   native Hebrew language. And this is not conversation, it is a proclamation.

Because to proclaim means to announce something officially or publicly—and to do it with authority! And when Peter heard the critical commentary of the spectators, he raised his voice and proclaimed:"Men of Judea and all who dwell in Jerusalem, let's get one thing straight—these men are not drunk as you suppose, but this is what was spoken by God through the prophet who said that 'In the last days, I will pour out my Spirit on all flesh and your sons and your daughters shall prophesy, your young men shall see visions, and your old men shall dream dreams. And whosoever shall call on the name of the Lord shall behaved!'"

This is the same Peter who at the judgment hall denied Christ, who is now declaring the Word of God as manifest in Christ. And he proclaims it publicly, officially, and with authority. Because when you understand ownership, it shows up not just in your conversation but also in your proclamation.

Have you ever noticed that when doctors speak, they speak with authority about what is wrong with your body and what can possibly be done to make you feel better? When economists speak they speak with authority about the market, inflation, and other projections. When athletes speak, they speak with authority about their sport. Even when idiots speak they do so with authority on idiocy. Liars speak with authority that's why other people believe their lies. Yet, it seems like when Christians speak, we speak with doubt, fear, and uncertainty. Perhaps this is because we don't want to offend anyone or say the wrong thing. But the text tells us that when you understand your ownership, you obtain the power of proclamation.

Proclaim justice will come for those who have been victimized by injustice. Proclaim that peace will come only after the demands of protesters have been heard and addressed. Proclaim the salvation of a nation only as it validates and hears the voices of all of its citizens. Proclaim restoration of rejoicing when victory has been won.

Ownership Changes the Source of your Celebration

The means through which God showed up in the upper room was not expected by anyone who was in the room. The expressed concern of the followers of Jesus was for the restoration of the Israel's independence. Perhaps they were expecting a military campaign, a political coup, an open rebellion against Roman rulers, armed conflict in capital cities. Fires burning down the symbols of their socio-economic oppression were expected. However, what they experience in that upper room is not what any of them expected. They did not expect the rushing wind, the tongues, of fire, or to hear the works of God in the various languages of the earth. They did not expect to discover that spiritual liberation was paramount to their social liberation. The resulting celebration in the room then is not that God did what they wanted God to do, in a manner that they expected God to do, but that God had done what God wanted to do.

For example, when we go on job interviews, we pray and ask God to give us the job. When we get turned down, we feel disappointment and defeat, as if our prayers did not work. Or when a loved one is sick, we pray for healing. Despite our prayers, however, sometimes the loved one dies. The assumption is that because God did not do what we wanted, in the manner that we expected, that either our prayers did not work or God failed to hear. However, the Pentecost narrative suggests that even if God does not do what we asked God to do, the way we expect God to do, we can still celebrate that God has done what God wanted to do.

We celebrate because God's will is not subject to our will. We celebrate because it's not our will, but God's will that must be done. We celebrate because the source of our celebration is not in what God has done, or has not done, but we celebrate God simply because God is God. As Vicki Yohe sang"

Because of who You are, I give you glory.
Because of who You are, I give you praise.
Because of who You are, I will lift my voice and say
'Lord I worship You because of who you are!'

Jehovah Jireh, my provider!
Jehovah Nissi, Lord You reign in victory!
Jehovah Shalom, my Prince of Peace!
Lord, I worship You because of who You are

Reignited for Revival
This is not a drill

Acts 2:14 -19; 37-39

Acts 2:14 Then Peter stood up with the Eleven, raised his voice and addressed the crowd: "Fellow Jews and all of you who live in Jerusalem, let me explain this to you; listen carefully to what I say.

15 These people are not drunk, as you suppose. It's only nine in the morning!

16 No, this is what was spoken by the prophet Joel:

17 "'In the last days, God says,
    I will pour out my Spirit on all people.
Your sons and daughters will prophesy,
    Your young men will see visions,
    Your old men will dream dreams.

18 Even on my servants, both men and women,
    I will pour out my Spirit in those days,
    And they will prophesy.

19 I will show wonders in the heavens above
    And signs on the earth below,
    Blood and fire and billows of smoke.

37 When the people heard this, they were cut to the heart and said to Peter and the other apostles, "Brothers, what shall we do?"

38 Peter replied, "Repent and be baptized, every one of you, in the name of Jesus Christ for the forgiveness of your sins. And you will

receive the gift of the Holy Spirit. 39 The promise is for you and your children and for all who are far off—for all whom the Lord our God will call."

In this the third part of the series Little Fires Everywhere, our text leads us from the initial outpouring of Holy Spirit to the holy boldness in which Holy Spirit operates within us. However, let's return to the literary text for a moment as we look at the mother Elena who's money, prestige and status cannot save her from the little fires she created… she has to come to grips with the reality that all of the trying to present a front of a perfect household and family has come to a tragic head… there are little fires everywhere burning down her grand house and she must finally face her role in the climate that brought about the dismantling of her family and the destruction of her home to this tragic place. Like this mother, America is in a similar predicament…institutionalized artificial fronts of United when clearly the divisions are evident is much like an infected sore that show no evidence of the infection inside until it is pressed and begins to ooze.., remember Hughes "Harlem: simile, deferred dreams that festers like a sore then run. There has always been a reason for protest, there has always been disparities, racism is far from new and it's entrenchment in the fabric of this country is not a stench that is Febreezable. The cover up won't work this time, There are little fires everywhere and they have brought the chickens home to roost… yes there have been protests before and they served as a precursor to the real thing and never taken seriously because there was no real threat. Let me paint a picture...

In every school, when I was teaching middle school, there were times of the year for practicing what to do if a fire was in the building. But sometimes pranks caused the fire alarm to be pulled, and it became so common that there was a desensitized feeling about alarms. But this is not a drill!

I was told a story about a school where the air conditioner was in a separate building in the back of the school and connected through a duct system. One day the air conditioner blew something and caught on fire. The fire came before alarm. In fact, my cousin whose class was near it. He saw it and called the office to sound the alarm. The children who had consistently kept playing during a drill, failed to respond until they saw the fire. When it became evident that this was not a drill, one child had seizure in the middle of chaos and reminds us that while the fires burn we are having a seizure called Covid 19, and we must care for ourselves and we must find a place of calm in the middle of the drama, despite the danger.

Like the fire in the back of the school that took time to manifest itself as a climate changing event…we are faced with a myriad of constantly rekindled fires everywhere and this is real…Church, we must be present and prepared to meet the challenges of this age cause we can't serve what we cannot see… we must cease to be surface in our prayers and hope this goes away. It's time to get up and move …cause here's the newsflash: This is not a drill!

Because it's not a drill we must be unafraid to speak truth to power in a prophetic way;

Prophetic Proclamation must be spoken…A Right now word in its season

.Peter prophetically reminds these good Jewish church folks of the prophecy…he could have ignored the shade driven "these are drunk" statement…but the words gave newly fire baptized Peter the boldness to set a little fire of his own…He says they are not drunk…but they are spirit filled…in fact I'm so woke in the spirit,,, let me tell you what you did to Jesus…and how that's gonna really backfire on you…cause this is not a drill! This is that day that Joel's prophecy comes to fruition! At that moment in time, Peter becomes the voice of the prophecy. It is important that we find our prophetic voice…so that like Issachar we can clearly assess the temperature, the pulse of the times, and speak to it! Like my cousin who clearly saw the path of the fire at the middle school long before it reached the building...we have to be in tune and speak to what we see...to join the prophets like Jeremiah, Habakkuk, Isaiah and Joel and recent historic ones, Dr. King Malcolm X, John Lewis, and yes Curtis Mayfield, Marvin Gay, Sweet Honey in the Rock, Bernice Reardon Johnson, and modern ones, yes. Tupac, Nipsey Hustle, Common and others whose words cry out to their generations in prophetic ways...We must see the fires...cry out not for someone to put them out...but for someone to just understand the flames and the why! This is not a drill!!!

Because this is not a drill there has to be some cause for the fire and we must do a thorough investigation of the reason for the fires … acknowledge where they start and then seek to correct the problem….

Penance must be preceded by penitence

Peter says repent and be baptized...

There is a difference between penance and penitence- At the end of the Little Fires Everywhere story, the mother who did not set the fire, takes the blame because she knows her ways, her manipulation, her forced facade of a life placed her family in a place the led to little fires everywhere...America has to experience penance...but it won't be useful until it also exhibits and commits to penitence...not only from the black lives that matter, but from the native American lives that matter. There are a plethora of reasons we are at this place… and each must be faced and not given a pass… I hear you saying, but Pastor we have to forgive, and yes we are mandated to do so, but that doesn't change the culpability of the guilty parties. In order to manage the fire…facing the elements that are the accelerant for the fire is imperative.

What most people want is a pass, and Passes are not being given right now and while somewhat to apply self inflicted penance, just penance for there are multiple resignation because of confessions of insensitivity. There are corporate statements of support...but much of it is still only about a bottom line and no penitence is involved. Without penitence the get on the BLM bandwagon act is a perfunctory rudimentary exercise in "my bad"!

The question in the text remains...the question by those who heard and were convicted by Peter was what shall we do? This is the place of contrition needed right now... Peter answers the question for those who will ...he answers the question for those who will listen today...he answers for governments for institutionalized racism, for unjust statues and for the church when it turns its head in resignation.

What shall we do...repent!...the church has some repenting to do as well for our inward focused and not enough care for others; our Matthew 25 "least for these" progress report has a failing percentage and we must face our role in the numbing of the people and the disregard for the plight of the disenfranchised ... and repent! Cause this is not a drill!

We have to be bold enough to speak prophetically we have to contrite enough to seek penance and penitence to be positioned to receive the Promise

Where we stand in our penitence and penance determines how we will be able to receive the promise....We have to be in posture to receive the promise...we have to be contrite in spirit to receive forgiveness...so that we can be recipients of the fullness of the Holy Spirit...and the text says that its generational -not a pass, but an exemplar from us to do likewise..

...It is an inheritance for those who will accept and say yes to the spirit's call and "Save yourselves from this untoward generation". Save yourself from the foolishness around us. Save yourself from always thinking what we have is more important than who we are Save yourself from celebritism that turns our head away from whets important. This is not a drill…The question is are we aware and engaged? or are drunk with the wine of the world as James Weldon Johnson wrote in lift every voice and sing…this is not a drill… we must serve this present age… not what we want it to be but what it is… yes people are angry, and unwilling to back off until justice is served … not just for one man or woman at a time but for everyone victimized.

This week at the funeral of George Floyd one of the most powerful moments was the presence of family members of other victims of unmerited death by law enforcement…the need to remember and never forget is fuel for the fire I didn't say don't forgive I said stay alert! And each time a new fire is lit, there is a wildfire effect. We must join others to strengthen the movement!!

Church we have been part of a liberation movement for over 2000 years, this movement is not antithetical to the cause of Christ. For Jesus is the great liberator! We must make sure our fires are still burning … we must stay connected to other little fires and be kingdom builders and warriors for justice at the same time… be evangelist and also missionaries… be praises and worshippers but also concerned about the plight of the people… we must be spiritual multi-taskers and be lights in darkness… we must not continue to be a once a week drill but to catch on fire!

We must catch on fire in our love for God and each other… because this is not a drill

We must be fires of hope….cause this is not a drill

Fires of truth- because this is not a drill

Fires of Justice- Cause this is not a drill

Unafraid, Boldly standing, and ready to do what is required of us.

To do justice and love, mercy and to walk humbly with God! - This is not a drill…

We must be willing to do what we must do to serve this present age ….not the one we want, but the one that is…

We have to be committed to a yes to all the spirit tells us when the Lord speaks in the power of the Holy Spirit we have to say yes…

Yes to his way , to his will, to his direction, Yes, I will speak Yes, I will pray Yes, I will go...There are little fires everywhere… and this not a drill! Can you say yes?!

Song of Decision- I'll Say Yes

(Sung by Shirley Caesar)

I'll say yes, Lord, yes

To your will and to your way

I'll say yes Lord yes I will trust you and obey

When your Spirit speaks to me with my whole heart I'll agree

And my answer will be yes, Lord, yes!

Third Sunday After Sunday

When Men Need a Move

And at this sound the crowd gathered and was bewildered.
Acts 2:6a

No one who has seen the miniseries "Little Fires Everywhere" could confuse the story and claim it is a story about men. As I have been sharing with you, it is a story about race and class. It is about politics and privilege; Motherhood, mistakes, and misery. It is a story about identity and history—ownership and oppression; control, chaos, and trying to keep it all together—that centers around women.

The women stand in the spotlight. The women are the feature and the focus. The female actresses and characters get the attention, the appreciation, and the accolades. And while I have no issue with that whatsoever, I do need to highlight how this phenomenon mirrors what many men are feeling this Father's Day. For while—in the words of James Brown—this is a man's world—and while patriarchy permeates everything from the Sacred Text to societal structures—no one can argue that the celebration of Father's Day pales in comparison to the celebration of Mother's Day.

Celebrate Men?

As one of our members pointed out, there were no Father's Day profile picture frames flooding Facebook like there was for Mother's Day. The aisles are never as packed with people buying Father's Day gifts as they were when people were even willing to risk catching COVID-19 to go out and buy Mother's Day gifts. There is no supply of sentimental songs celebrating fathers, no deluge of day-long tributes to dads for all that they do, no outpouring of ostentatious accolades for the men who have made meaningful contributions to our lives like we do for our moms. No, no, no—when it comes to these particular holidays, mothers get first class treatment, and fathers get it second-class—low class—or no class treatment.

And no matter how macho we may act, ladies, men like tube acknowledged and appreciated just like you do. No matter how stubborn we may be, men want to be supported and celebrated just like you do. We may not be able to do the things that you do, or go through the same troubles that you do, with the style and grace that you do but we are dealing with the fears, the failures, and the frustrations of life too.

Again, I was reminded of this as I revisited the characters and events of "Little Fires Everywhere."For while the women are rightly and understandably the stars of the story, the men who occupy the story's subtext also have some struggles. I'm not just talking about Bill—the husband of Elena—who lives repressing the memory and the meaning of how his wife spent the night out with an ex-boyfriend 15 years ago because she was not satisfied with the life he was trying to provide former, but the Black men in the story have some serious struggles too. Joseph Ryan—the man who is mesmerized with Mia on the subway and who eventually works up the nerve to ask Mia to be a surrogate for him and his wife because his wife is unable to reproduce. While Mia agrees to the arrangement, she later takes off with the baby she is carrying—and Joseph never sees the child he fathered.

Brian is the Black athlete and high school senior with hopes of going to Princeton. He likes his White girlfriend—who happens to be Elena's daughter—but he is torn by the way she appropriates Black culture and steals an essay written by Pearl—Mia daughter—in order to boost her application to Yale. Brian loves having sex with Lexie—his White girlfriend—but when Lexie fantasizes aloud about having a baby with him—because unbeknownst to him, she's actually pregnant—Brian responds that he doesn't want to be "that guy—(as in) another Black kid who knocked up a girl before he even graduated."

Then, there is Warren—Mia's younger brother—who is killed in a car accident at 17 years old. Warren's death, in part, motivates Mia to begin her nomadic lifestyle and keep her daughter's paternity a secret. The women may be the ones in the spotlight of the series, but the men—especially the Black men in the story—are having some serious struggles too.

Black Men Are in Trouble Today

Like Joseph, we sometimes have strained relationships (or no relationship) with our children, not because we don't want it, but because someone is intentionally keeping us apart. Like Brian, we, too, have hopes, goals, and dreams that have been hindered and hung up but hurts, grief, and difficult decisions. We, too, enjoy the experiences of sexuality, but don't always exercise the necessary accompanying responsibility. Like Warren, we, too, are being taken away by tragedy before we truly get a chance to know and experience what life is all about.

We are dealing with COVID-19 on one hand, and cops killing us on the other hand. We are participating in protests some days and being victimized by White privilege every day. We are mistreated, mistrusted, and misused. We're being burdened on one hand by a world blaming us for its troubles and burdened on the other hand by women disappointed that we can't always be the men they want and need us to be. We are increasingly being unjustly incarcerated and tragically miseducated. We are trying to externally hold it together, when we are falling apart. We are putting up the façade of being strong, when inside we feel weak.

And people wonder why we are often moody and mannish— why we act angrily and aggressively—why we have a higher likelihood of having heart attacks—why we are quiet and keep so much stuff to ourselves—it's because we don't know who to trust and where to turn so others won't take advantage of us. In other words, we are in a place of frustration, agitation, and stagnation— and we need a move! We need a move that will turn confusion into clarity, obstructions into opportunities, and struggles into strength. We need a move that will turn ambition into action, failures into fearlessness, and plans into purpose.

That's where the men whom we meet in Acts 2 are, and have been, in our text—they are men who need a move. They are repressed men who live under Roman authority, oppressed men live in an occupied country, and hated men who have been hurt and hung by the lack of justice in the justice system. For remember with me who is present in the nucleus of the group that meets in the Upper Room of Acts 2.At the nucleus of the group are 11 men who dedicated the last three years of their lives to following Jesus and trying to make a difference. They left the close quarters of family trying to forge a better future for their families. They have sacrificed personal safety for long term security.

Around this core group of 11 remaining disciples, are other men who had also followed Jesus, just like the 11remaining disciples did, but none of those men—except Matthias—ever got an official title. The Bible says that altogether there were about 120 of them. They had seen the Difference-Maker die, the Favored One fall, their Savior secured in a tomb. Three days later, Jesus, the Reason for their Rejoicing, was resurrected—and for the next 40 days everything seemed fine. Then they saw Him catch a cloud and disappear from their sight.

Now, for ten days, they have been wanting something to happen, needing something to happen, and waiting for something to happen. They need a move from God to make sense of the messes of their lives. They need a move from God to change the atmosphere and   their attitudes. They need a move from God to make a way, to work a miracle; to give them might, to mandate a mission. And for those today, who are looking for meaning, or who need God to make a way, Acts 2 gives good news.

When Men Need a Move, God Makes a Move

The truth of the text is not only applicable to men, but since it's Father's Day, I'm saying "men "but the truth of the text is applicable to women and children too].

For the text says "suddenly they heard a sound from heaven as of a rushing mighty wind."That's what the English says. The English says "suddenly they heard a sound from heaven." However, that's not exactly how the Greek says it. In the Greek, the word we translate "suddenly" is taken from the Greek *aphno*. *Aphno* means unexpectedly. It means to shock or to surprise because there is no expectation. So even though over 120 people have been in this upper room for ten days—praying and petitioning God and being on one accord with each other—nobody in the room was expecting God to move the way God moved.

I wonder if there's anybody listening who knows what it means to needing God to do something, wanting God to do something, praying for God to do something, and then when God actually does it, it catches you by surprise? Have you ever found ourselves saying "I asked God to bless me, but didn't know He was going to bless me *like that*? I asked God to make a way for me, but I didn't know He was going to make it *like that*? I asked God to take care of my enemies, but I didn't know He was going to do it *like that*? You see, Beloved, you can be *expecting* God to do *something*, but when God shows up, He can do it income unexpected ways.

I don't know *what* God is going to move but when a man needs a move, God makes a move. I don't know *where* God is going to move but when a man needs a move, God makes a move. I don't know *when* God is going to move but when a man needs a move, God makes a move. I don't know *who* God is going to move but when a man needs a move, God makes a move. I don't know *why* God is going to move but when a man needs a move, God makes a move. I don't know *how* God is going to move but when a man needs a move, God makes a move. And when God makes a move, He is able to do exceedingly and abundantly above all we can ask or think!

Again, the text says "suddenly—*aphno*—unexpectedly they heard astound."   That's what the English says. The English says suddenly they heard a sound. But the Greek doesn't say they heard a sound. The Greek says *aphno*—unexpectedly—*echos*—sound. *Aphnoechos*: suddenly or unexpectedly there was sound. Not "they heard" just unexpectedly there was sound. In the Greek text, it is not important that the people in the upper room heard the sound; in the Greek text it is only important that there was a sound.

In other words, whether they heard it or not, God was there making a move. Whether they acknowledged it or not, God was there making a move. Whether they received it or not, God was there making a move. Understand, even if you don't hear what God is saying, God is speaking. You may not see what God is doing, but God is up to something. You may not know which way God is going, but God is moving. Your perception of God neither limits nor stops the action or ability of God.

Sometimes you can't even see what God is doing until it's already done. Sometimes you can't even see that God is present until the moment has passed. Sometimes you can't hear what God is saying until after everything is silent. But if you ever doubt God's ability to unexpectedly do whatever needs to be done, let me ask you a common quadruplet of questions: has God ever made a way when you didn't have a dime? Has God ever stepped in just right on time? Has God ever picked you up when you were down? Has God ever placed your feet on solid ground? Then you know He is a Rock in a weary land and a shelter in the time of storm. And you know that whenever you need a move, God makes a move!

God Tells You What the Move Means

While the Greek text does not emphasize the importance of the people who were in the upper room hearing a sound, in verse 6, of Acts 2, there is an emphasis on the fact that folks who were not in the room both heard sound and came to see what was happening at its source. And when the multitude of men from throughout the city arrived, they heard Galileans speaking about the wonderful works of God in the various languages of the land. Verse 12 says they were all amazed and perplexed, saying to one another "Whatever could this mean?"Some of the men in the crowd begin to say "it means they are drunk and full of new wine."Verse 14 says "But Peter stood up, with the eleven, and raised his voice saying these men are not drunk, but this is what was spoken of by the prophet Joel."

The text, then, is trying to tell us today, that when God makes a move, some people will mock you and make fun of you. Some will misunderstand both you, and what God is doing for you. Some will poke, prod, and pick at you, but no matter how much they may mistreat you, when God moves, God will tell you what the move means. The mockers thought it was a new thing, but Peter stood up and said "No this means that God is fulfilling some old things."The mockers misunderstood and made fun, but Peter stood up and said "This is not funny; this is the fruit of being faithful."The mockers were being entertained by the show, but Pete stood up and said "This is not a show, this is God showing up!"

How does this textual detail connect to events we see unfolding in 2020? The protests taking place in the street—it's God showing   up! The world citizens speaking out against racism and White privilege—it's God showing up! Little fires everywhere—it's God showing up! The emptiness of Trump's rally yesterday in Tulsa—it's God showing up! The expanded awareness of Juneteenth—it's God showing up! Because when men need a move, God will make the move, and then tells you what the move means.

Noah, God will make the move and tell you to build an ark, and then tell you it means it's going to rain. Moses, God will make the move and spare your life from genocide, then tell you it means you're going to lead enslaved people to liberty. Jonah, God will make the move and have a fish swallow you up, then tells you it means you're going to preach whether you want to or not. David, God will make the move and anoint you with oil, and then tells you it means you're going to be a king. Hosea, God will make the move and tell you to faithfully marry and unfaithful woman, then tell you it means that's how faithful I am to my unfaithful people. Simon, God will make the move and change your name to Peter then tells you it means upon this rock I will build my church.

We may not fully understand the meaning of what we experience while we're experiencing it, but we'll understand it better by and by.

Now It's Your Move

The same men who came to make fun went from asking "What does this mean" to asking "What shall we do?" Because whenever God starts doing something, it requires and elicits a response. Whenever the word of God is proclaimed, it elicits a response of acceptance or rejection. And so these were men who needed a move and God showed up and made a move, then God explained what the move meant. Then God steps back and says "Now it is your move." All I can do is tell you the truth but I cannot make you accept the truth. All I can do is reveal my will, but I cannot make you rejoice in doing my will.

And so then my brothers, and my sisters, I hear God say now it's your move. After all of your protesting and picketing, looting and your rioting, complaining and criticizing, I hear God saying I made My move, not it is your move. Now it your move to stand up and be the men I have call you to be! It is your move to protest all the way to the ballot box and let your voices be heard through your votes. It is your move to tear down the old way in order to work with Me to show the world a more excellent way. We can't simply sit back and watch God move, but God says now it is your move.

But I hear somebody say that the task is too great. The challenge is too great; it is too large. God may be on our side, but it seems like there is nothing more we can do. In response, I offer the point of a story I once heard told by Dr. Jeremiah Wright. The story is of a painting that depicts a man playing chess with the devil. The devil has a lot of pieces left on the board while the man only has four or five pieces on the board. The painting is called "Checkmate," as it depicts that the devil is poised to declare that the game is over and he is victorious.

One day a tour was going through the museum, and as the tour guide led attendees through the museum, they came to the painting—"Checkmate"—looked at it for a while, then moved on to see other painting in the museum. However while the group moved on, one man lingered behind, staring at "Checkmate." Sometime later, when the tour group had moved into the final gallery of the tour, the man who had stayed behind came running through the halls of the museum shouting "it's a lie! It's a lie! It's not checkmate! The devil may have all the pieces, and the many playing against him may only have four pieces, but it's not checkmate!"

What nobody else in the group knew was that the man who had lingered behind staring at "Checkmate"—who was now running through the museum screaming "it's a lie"—was a Russian Chess Master. As such he could see what nobody else in the group could see. As a Chess Master, he could something that even the artist of the picture couldn't see. After examining the painting, and the chess pieces and positions depicted on the board, and applying his knowledge of chess rules and strategy, the Chess Master could see the man depicted playing chess with the devil was not checkmated, because he still had his "king" chess piece on the board, and his kin had another move!

I came to tell somebody that it may look like you're backed up into a corner. It may look like the devil has you checkmated. I may look like the system built against you is about to destroy you. But there is a King on your side, and your King has another move. Your King can still make a way. There is a King who rules heaven and earth. And He knows just how much you can bear!

Restricted Respiration...We need Pneuma

John 20:21-22; Acts 2:1-4; 40-41

As we come to the end of this series of sermons Little Fires Everywhere: Reignited for Revival, let me return once more to the literary text/ series one last time...The buildup of circumstances that caused the fires came from choices, and while most of the focus is on the women (the mothers in this story. and their children) there are men, two in particular. They are static characters who are supporting characters, but they are important to the underline story, as they are the fathers of the young people in the story. One is married to Elena the fake perfectionist. The other is Mya's "arrangement," an answer to a fertility problem between him and his wife, and though she accepted the proposition to be the surrogate, she reneges and steals the baby, who is now in high school. While Bill, the husband of Elena, deals with his own issues in relation to his marriage, It is Pearl's father particularly as a black man that represents the difficulty of respiration in a world that easily writes off black fathers, and never questions where he is or why he is not involved in his daughters life.

Far too many men in this culture can't breathe not just because of the looming threat of assumed quilt because of skin color...not just because of the seeming reemergence of yesteryear hangings...or because of the fear of getting stopped by law enforcement and inadvertently making a wrong move, or saying the wrong thing that gets you dead. Black men can't breathe because life as a black man has always caused restricted respiration...expectation low...accusations high...constantly in a state of prove yourself...and far too often your best is not good enough. Does that excuse those who fail to live up to the standard, no, but history, cultural disparity, and the lack of role models have contributed to the problem of respiration for African American men, and it has had a ricochet effect on African Americans everywhere….Kermit the frog, of Muppet fame sings a song that states it's not that easy being green...well it's not easy, in fact it abundantly difficult being black African American in a country that has never appreciated you- that does not see you. In a country where you are an addendum, a back drop, a prop, an overly generalized episode in American life, and where your life does not matter. That's why this movement is combustible...That's why little fires are everywhere. The fires are an awakening, and where there is fire there is smoke. Smoke inhalation is leading cause of death in fires. Most people don't die from getting burned; they die because they can't breathe…they die because of restricted respiration.

The word respirator, in its medical senses, dates back to around 1785–95. Respirator, respiratory, and respiration all derive from the Latin verb respīrāre, "to breathe, breathe out." When respiration is restricted we can't breathe! The word for breath is pneuma.   It is the root word for the respiratory disease pneumonia...which is a lung disease that makes it hard to breathe...Covid 19 often attacks the lungs often manifesting as pneumonia and makes breathing difficult…

Our pericope for today's message looks at the Holy Spirit as Jesus announces his "save the unknown date" arrival post-resurrection and how the Spirit will manifest as the promise post ascension. Our text also explores what Holy Spirit produces. I want to suggest to you that there is a spiritual correlation between all of the breathing difficulties in life and living coming into view simultaneously in this season…

Covid19...we can't breathe

Knees on necks...we can't breathe

Hangings in multiple places...we can't breathe

Disproportionate health care cost and availability--- we can't breathe

Food deserts that limit oxygenated foods....we can't breathe

Educational system lacking...we can't breathe

Racial unrest, president speaking venom, colliding ideology ...we can't breathe

We are living every day with Traumatic Stress Disorder...cause Post never comes...we can't breathe...

And in order to catch our breath and to breathe completely, we must receive and employ the Holy Spirit to provide breath... pneuma for our faith, for our fight for justice, and for our future

Restricted Respiration: We need Pneuma!

Jesus breathed on them...preparation for the promise APRs

The two main types are air-purifying respirators (APRs) and supplied-air respirators (SARs).

When Jesus offered them peace and breathed on them in John's account, is was like a respirator...it was not a ventilator because they were not filled...They received the filter that prepared them for the infilling...they received the foretaste to the glory in store...they received the precursor to the transformation... they got a hint, an appetizer of the mighty power to come!

While the breath of Jesus is a foretaste of what's to come...In our culture the respirator for our restricted respiratory as related to justice is not really a foretaste, but a stop gap. It is holidays acknowledged, CEOs resigning, a Netflix black lives matter line up, podcasts thrown together to give a nod to the movement, but yet not be moved. Just like wearing a mask: it helps but only if you wear it, and only if you stay socially distanced. It doesn't require great investment and it doesn't change much. The culture has been offering respirators for decades, but it's not willing to even offer effective PPE for our lives. Every now and then someone comes up with a viable short term non-destructive program that helps like a cultural CPAP machine that unfortunately is only of use while we are sleeping and if not cleaned out often will cause infection and can kill us.

The breath of Jesus on the disciples prepared them for that which was to come...gave them peace and a proclamation...receive the Holy Spirit...as we seek to breathe, we must receive the Holy Spirit and know that while we fight ...while we live in uncertainty, it is the pnuema of Christ that will keep us until we can harness the power of the promise.

Wind came and filled them- promises made, promises kept

(SARs).

When the wind came, it was mighty and rushing, not gentle. It moved all who were in proximity, all who were near. It was an infiltration! The spirit Jesus had breathed on them was now in them. Much like a ventilator, a SAR is a stream of constantly flowing air. The Holy Spirit filled those in the house and gave them the fulfillment of the promise from Jesus. This wind, this infilling, provided those who received it with fire...that landed on them...the fire of boldness... to speak in ways that they could be heard and understood.

In this climate, we have to be unafraid of the mighty and the rushing...and of the wind of change that is infiltrating. We can't be in love with the past and miss the promise of the future. We must catch on fire, and stay lit knowing that the Holy Spirit is working within us; pnuema within us to guide, to lead, to teach, to speak, to grow, to fight, and to shape us. When we do, respiration will no longer be restricted in our spirit, and the pneuma within us, can affect the restricted respiration in the culture, in the nation, among our people,

and even the world! We need Pneuma!!!

Presence of Holy Spirit moved them- Promise was fulfilled and provided the church with power-filled purpose

Peter said save yourself from this corrupt generation, corrupt meaning "perverse, unfair, and unjust". Church, we must harness the breath of Holy Spirit to operate in power; power to walk in our purpose and power to speak truth even when it's uncomfortable. Power to stand for right when everyone is wrong; power to push back against negativity; power to diffuse cultural and spiritual low self worth and esteem; power to stop being in the shadows. Power to stop ignoring each of our contributions to this transformation...Power to stop being benign and in the shadows when we are called to be out front and power to avoid pimping people and being pimped...

We have to be careful not to be like the story of a woman who knew there were problems all around her life. She kept going and never acknowledged them. One day a close friend asked her why she never looks at the truth of her life. Her response was "if I look at it I may have to do something about it" the power of the Holy Spirit gives us the courage to look and to do something. Power gives us what we need to do all we have been assigned to do for the kingdom and to fulfill the Great Commission!

What will we do differently...We can't do what we've always done because we will keep getting what we've always gotten. We must harness the real power of the pnuema of Holy Spirit, not the pie in the sky opiate of shouting our troubles over, not the by and by when the morning comes, great getting up morning resolve of yesteryears, but that which is the *dunamis*, the dynamite power of the breath of Holy Spirit on us and in us to change the scope of life and living and to help us to be that change!

We must expect the power to breathe on us, to breathe in us, and fill us.

We need Pnuema.

Pnuema will wake us up...

Pneuma will help us stand

Pneuma will lift us up

Pneuma will transform us, translate us, and transport us, to a place where God can use us for his glory...in the church...in the streets...and in the world!

There are little fires everywhere and the smoke before and after the fires have us gasping for air, and in the natural, we can't breathe. But there is a breath, the breath of the Holy Spirit that will open the airways of our lives, open the air passages of our spirit, and breathe new life within us! Breath Holy Spirit...Breathe Holy Spirit ....Breathe!!

Song of Decision: Fill Me up - Jesus Culture

You provide the fire

And I'll provide the sacrifice

You provide the spirit

And I will open up inside

Fill me up, God

Fourth Sunday After Pentecost

Who Started the Fire?

*Now when they heard this, they were cut to the heart and
said… 'What should we do?'*
Acts 2:37

"Little Fires Everywhere" begins with the Richardson house already on fire. Flames are shooting through the roof. Dark smoke is billowing into the sky. The whole house is engulfed, and the house is burning down. In the aftermath, the fire chief walks up to Elena Richardson—the mother of the family who lives in the house—and says to her that the fire was an act of arson. Someone intentionally started the fire and used an accelerant to ensure the fire spread quickly. And when the fire chief asks Mrs. Richardson if she knew who started the fire, Elena says "I did it."That's how the story begins; it begins with Elena saying "I did it. I started the fire."

However, when you get to the end of "Little Fires Everywhere, "and see the events that occur immediately before the fire began, it is plain to see that Elena did not really start the fire. It is not her idea. She does not know that it was about to happen. She neither purchased nor provides the accelerant. She does not pour it in the various rooms. She does not strike the match. As a matter of fact, Elena is in a different part of the house altogether when the fires start. Yet at the beginning of the story when the fire chief asks Elena who started the fire she says "I did it."

And as we watch Elena confess to starting the fire, that she, existentially, did not start, many of us watching the miniseries are confused, but for Elena it is a moment of clarity. For when Elena confesses to burning down her own house what she is saying is "I may not be the culprit, but I am culpable. I may not have struck the match but I sat at the helm of the system. I may not be immediate the cause, but I instigated the cause. I may not have participated in it, but

I am the person behind it. I created the atmosphere. I overlooked dangerous signs. I ignored those who were insulted and injured by my inaction and inattentiveness."In other words, Elena "confession "is as admission that while she may not have purposefully started the fire, she passively participated in other people's persecution which precipitated the fire. She failed to protect people who were vulnerable from being victimized, while simultaneously propagating the pain and persecution of those same unprotected people. Hence, she was just as guilty and just as culpable as the people who poured the accelerant, and struck the match, and directly started the fire.

White people and people in positions of power today would do well to experience Elena's epiphany. Because as dissatisfaction with the status quo evinces itself in the little fires burning everywhere today, privileged people and people in power are quick to claim that the fires are not their fault. They are quick to claim that they are not racist. Or they don't see color. Or the only color that matters is green. They are quick to say that they have a friend who is Black; or they never owned slaves; or they voted for Obama as if their passiveness, their progressiveness, their political correctness, or the passage of time somehow placates the pain of oppressed people.

Elena's epiphany about how her ignorance and lack of involvement led to the fires that burned down her house could be informative for passive and privileged people trying to make sense of the fires that are burning today.   Personally, you may have never owned a slave, but you still benefit from the systems of antebellum and post-Modern slavery. You may not use the "N" word, but you also don't say a darn word when unarmed Black and Latino people are killed by White vigilantes and law enforcement officials. You claim you don't see race, so you act like you can't see the disproportionate number of Blacks who are intentionally undereducated, unjustly incarcerated, inaccurately delineated, and hated because we are melanated.

These Fires Are Your Fault

You are not as blind to these abuses as you pretend to be. You are not as ignorant about these issues as you claim to be. You are not as innocent in these injustices as you wish you could be. So don't blame the Black protesters in the *streets* for the little fires burning everywhere, blame the racists who no longer have to hide under white sheets. Don't blame the people with raised fists, chanting "no justice, no peace," blame the keepers of the status quo who have given us no other choice. Don't point the finger blaming men and women who look like me, look in the mirror and blame people who look like you. You are the ones who enkindled these issues. You are the ones who caused this chaos. You are the ones who prompted these protests. And you are the ones who need to come to your senses, confess your complicity, and cooperate with those of us calling for the country to be more racially accepting, ethnically inclusive, economically equitable, and intolerant of injustice. Because whether you like it or not, these fires are your fault!

And that is exactly what Peter tells the people who showed up on the day of Pentecost. They wanted to distance themselves from the source of the spectacular scene they were seeing but Peter tells theme in the crowd you started this fire! You who are laughing and making light of this move of the Spirit of the Lord—you started these fires. You who overlook and oppress children as too young adwoman as weak—you started these fires. You who senselessly support systems of slavery and say it is God's will—you who do not heed the Word of God and deny the works of the Son of God—you who wanted Jesus beaten and worked for the release of Barabbas— you who crucified Christ to maintain corruption—you who denied the One who came to deliver—

You are the ones who started this fire.

So when you show up and see the fires today, know that these fires are the result of what you did 53 days ago when you watched Jesus is lynched. These fires today are the result of what your parents and grandparents, and great grandparents have been doing for generations—ignoring the prophets sent by God. These fires today are the result of systems of racism, sexism, and oppression that your ancestors built and from which you still benefit. This is God letting you know that the Word you did not heed—the Messenger that you mistreated—the Christ whom you crucified, God has made Him both Lord and Christ. You tried to throw Him aside, but God was (and still is) on His side!

Oftentimes it is hard for people who think they are innocent to accept that they are guilty. It is hard for people who point an accusatory finger at you, to realize that the other three fingers of that same hand are incriminatingly pointing back at them. That, my friends, is why many of us have never received and apology that we were owed or deserved. That is why some relationships that were broken have never been finished, even though they could have been salvaged. Because oftentimes people would rather walk away than admit that they were wrong.

However, the text says in Acts 2:37, that when the crowd heard the words of Peter, "they were cut to the heart."That's why the protesters have got to keep protesting because when the crowd—the fire starters—heard the words of Peter "they were cut to the heart."That's why preachers have got to keep preaching the gospel of justice and liberation because when the crowd of fire starters—heard the words of Peter, "they were cut to the heart."

Cut—from the Greek word—*kataponeo*—means to vex, to oppress, or to weigh down with toil. They were *kataponeo* in their heart. Heart" from the Greek word *kardia*—meaning the essential part of one's being. *Kardia* is one's thoughts and feelings—that which is in the middle or the center or the core of one's being. When they heard the words of Peter, they were *kataponeokardia*—they were vexed or weighed down in their innermost parts. They were moved. They were affected. They were shaken to their core. A change occurred in them that were not a change of their minds, but it was a change in their hearts. The text, then is teaching us something about the very people who started the fire in this text, in Celeste Ng's work, and in our present world.

The Fire-Starters Need a Change of Heart

When the fire-starting spectators arrived on the scene, their minds were already made up. They had made up their minds that the followers of Jesus were drunk. They had made up their minds that scene was confusing, chaotic, and comical. They had already made up their minds that the people already in the room were either stupid or silly. And that the violence that they were seeing needed to stop.

Today's fire-starting spectators have already made up their minds that Black Lives Matter is unacceptable and that "All Lives Matter" is the only acceptable words to say. They have already made up their minds that their understanding is the right understanding and anybody who does not agree with them is wrong. Their minds are already made up that they—who immigrated to this country themselves—needed to "Make America Great Again," and anybody who complains about America need to go back to Africa, or wherever else they had come from. Their minds are made up, but when they heard the words of Peter, they can very well be*kataponeokardia*—vexed in their hearts.

I need us to understand that it is a change of heart that God is calling for in the eruption of little fires everywhere. God is not trying to change minds; God is trying to   change hearts. This is the mistake that many of us make when we misunderstand the difference between what happens in John 21, and Acts 2.Over the years, I have heard I hear preachers and church people erroneously claim that the followers of Christ received the gift of the Holy Ghost in John 21 when Jesus breathed on them and said "receive the Holy Ghost."In John 21 Jesus blew on them—the Greek is *emphusao*. It means just what the English translates it to mean. It means Jesus blew on the surface or on the exterior of his followers. But what happens in Acts 2 is not *emphusao*—external—rather it is *kathizo*. *Kathidzo* comes from another Greek word which means to form a new base or foundation. It means to settle, or tarry, or dwell.

The difference between John 21 and Acts 2.John 21 was a foretaste, but in Acts 2, God is establishing a new foundation. John 21 is external, Acts 2 is internal. In John 21, God was changing the disciples' minds, but enacts 2; God is changing the people's hearts. And when the people in the Upper Room on Pentecost, experience being *kataponeokardia*—when they are pressed upon their hearts— they can no longer feel like they used to feel. They cannot think like they used to think. They can no longer act like they used to act. A change has taken place in the innermost parts of their being.

Psychologists work to change minds and ways of thinking, but only God can change your hearts. Pills can be prescribed to change mood and ways of feeling, but only God can change your heart. Plastic surgeons alter features and physical appearances, but only God can change your heart. When God changes your heart, some of the things you used to do, you won't do anymore. Some of the ways you used to think, you won't think anymore. Some of the things you used to feel, you won't feel anymore. You know how the hymnist exclaims "What a wonderful change in my life has been wrought since Jesus came into my heart!"The fire starters had made a choice in their heads, but God gave them a change in their hearts!

Fire-starters can make a Better Choice for their Children

When the people heard Peter preach, not only were they pricked to their hearts, but they asked Peter "what shall we do?" Peter replies in verse 38, "repent and be baptized for the remission of sins and you will receive the Holy Ghost."Then, note verse 39: "For the promise of God is to you and to your children!"The power of God is available to you and to your children. The peace of God is available to you and to your children. The protection of God is available to you and to your children. The blessings of God are not only available to you; they are also available to your children.

Your children will inherit the legacy that you leave. Your legacy is not only your land, it's also who and what you love. Your children will bear whatever you bequeath totem. That's not only what you buy but it's also your burdens. So when they ask Peter what to do, he reminds them that the decision they make today, will affect their children tomorrow. Do you want your children to fight the same battles fight that your parents before you fought—and you are fighting right now? Do you want your children to bear the same burdens that your parents before you bore—and you are bearing right now? Do you want your children to harbor the same hatred that your parents before you bore—and you are bearing right now?

The choices you make today, will affect your children, your community, the country, and the world tomorrow. In response, then, it you continue making the same choices generations before you made, your children and the world will only get more of what we've already gotten. It is time to a better future. God's promises are not on your past, but God's promises are on your future. God's provisions are not for your past but for your future. God purpose is not for your past but for your future. God's plans and not for your past but for your future.

When God says "I know the plans I have for you saith the Lord, plans to prosper you and give you peace"—that's a not a plan for your past, but a plan for your future. When the scripture asks "Is any among you sick"—not just physically sick, but spiritually sick? If any among you is sick, then let him pray and call on the elders of the church to anoint the sick one with oil, and the one who is sick shall recover—that's a promise on your future. "He will keep you in perfect peace"—that's a promise on your future. "He who begun a good work in you will perform it until it is complete"—that's a promise on your future.

Fire starters can be converted by its flames.

By the time Peter finished preaching in the Upper Room, three thousand of the critical and comedic spectators who showed up in the space were converted to being followers of Christ. Three thousand spectators got their own relationship with the Savior. Three thousand people, who just came to watch, found themselves being put to work! The same critics did not understand initially become allies. The same comedians who initially called the scene silly become its supporters. The same critics who initially complained begin to cooperate. They came comedians who initially laughed and what God was doing come to love what God is doing. They were converted by the flames of little fires burning everywhere. In like manner persons feeling the heat of today's fires—calling for social and systemic justice can be converted by the flames.

Epilogue:
Why The Fires Will Continue...

Waiting no more...the time is now!

401 years ago African Americans arrived on these shores and the diabolical institution of slavery which morphed from a labor experiment to a serial intentionally dehumanizing, disregarding, stereotyping , murdering, hate ridden generationally reinforced mindset that has so infiltrated the very fiber of America, that it has taken an "enough is enough" diverse grass roots movement to even get those who are the beneficiaries of the ingrained mindset and its economic benefits to even consider what has been perpetrated for 400 plus years.

For those who thought that electing an African American president was the recompense (Moscow Mitch) for the systemic ways in which those whose fore parents were slaves in this country are treated to this day, you are categorically mistaken. The election of Barrack Hussein Obama was a collective choice, but did not obliterate the system of racism, and while he was able to achieve this pinnacle, his status did not and does not excuse or allow for a misconstrued judgment on those in the African American community who have not been given the same opportunities, or who have been blocked, misguided, and dismissed by bigoted educators, racist officials and employers, and yes those in the religious community who have consistently misinterpreted biblical text for political gain.

This protest and subsequent response to the death of George Floyd and others is not an "all of sudden" phenomena. It has been bubbling for decades like a fire ready to combust. The cries of mistreatment have been ignored and disregarded....the pain of unmerited death by those sworn to protect and serve "all people" continues even in the midst of protest...the wealth disparity which results in a lack of basic needs, including living in food deserts and a lack of quality health care have contributed to the disproportionate occurrence of the deadly Covid-19 and its effect on African Americans.

These tangible issues along with the ever present undercurrent of assumptions of diminished intelligence, age old stereotypical expectations of character and integrity deprivation, and the ever present adages of "not good enough, not smart enough, not attractive enough" have added fuel to the "no more" resolve of African Americans. The struggle of waking up Black in America has activated the masses, especially the young who are not willing to fall victim to the "wait" posture of older generations. For Black Lives Matters, Color of Change, and other groups that are crossing racial demographics, the time is now! No more waiting, no more talking and doing little, and while the tenets of faith have a place, these groups are not waiting for a preacher to lead them...they are not interested in diffusing the anger with Hallelujahs, or initiating the olive branch, they are demanding intuition by the perpetrator...and until penitence, and reparations are evident and until there is substantive change...there will be no calm...No Justice No Peace.

Here's the truth...this time had to come. There was no avoiding it especially in an overt racist Trumpian environment. The infection has never been healed, only bandaged while still hurting. The scab of Civil Rights has never been fused into the skin of America, and the sore stays raised. Only when the perfunctory rudimentary (going through the motions) acts give way to real acknowledgment and repentance, with action, will America ever hope to be the United States...in fact, it needs to cease from using that erroneous description until it resembles the truth.

America, God's grace which is sung about (America the beautiful) has been cheapened by the inability or the lack of desire to see and acknowledge the sins of white fore parents as slave owners and rapists, and capitalist pimps...by the cheering of the masses as multiple persons were lynched merely because of their heritage...by the twisting of scripture to uphold the dehumanizing of persons throughout its history...by the institutionally driven profiling of African American men as probably criminal, no matter their status, by the over-sexualization of African American women, by zoning and city planning that allows food deserts to make quality food inaccessible for many neighborhoods, by substandard health care, if available at all, and by the reduced expectation of educational systems that position African American children to underachieve continuing the vicious cycle of poverty and disenfranchisement.

For those who ask what do they want? Let's start with the above mentioned issues. Then maybe we can sit at the table and figure out if "United" is attainable...but until then we will protest, plan, push policy, and yes pray...simultaneously! We are skilled, capable, astute and angry enough that backing down is not an option...waiting is a hard no...The time is now...pay attention!

Originally published in The Bright Star, African American publication in the Lufkin Daily News